DON'T MAKE A FUSS

It's only the Claremont Serial Killer

DON'T MAKE A FUSS

It's only the Claremont Serial Killer

A MEMOIR BY WENDY DAVIS

FREMANTLE PRESS

This book is dedicated, with sympathy and understanding, to the victims of the Claremont serial killer, their families, and their loved ones.

CONTENTS

Preface

It has now been more than thirty years since I was randomly, terrifyingly and without warning attacked in my Perth workplace by a man I didn't know, but who would become publicly known, some two-and-a-half decades later, as the Claremont serial killer.

Until an unexpected phone call from Western Australia police at my current home in Hobart some twenty-five years after the attack, I hadn't thought about it in years. Never for one moment had I considered writing about it. It was something that had happened to me – something so frightening that, wanting to eliminate the feelings of terror, helplessness, despair, shock and anger that had assailed me at the time, I had buried deep in my subconscious. Because it seemed to have been so easily forgotten by all those involved at the time – all except me – I had forced the trauma deep down. As people, especially women, of my time were taught to do, I just 'got on with it'. I didn't make a fuss.

But then, with that out-of-the-blue phone call from police investigating the Claremont killings, what happened to me all those years ago on the other side of the country came back with a vengeance, causing much turmoil in my life as it played itself out in what became a long and drawn-out sequel laced with anxiety, tragedy and sorrow.

A few of the people who witnessed this turmoil – including Cassandra, a counsellor with the Victims of Crime Unit in Hobart – suggested that it might be good therapy for me to document the events that had happened at the time of the attack itself, as well as what was happening currently and the impacts of it all. So I started to do this, using a pen and notebook, and during those early weeks as memories resurfaced and I woke in the night recalling vivid details from the past, I filled scraps of paper with words and sentences – rememberings of isolated incidents that sometimes didn't make much sense when I read them the next day, little scrambled jottings consisting mostly of intense feelings that overwhelmed me as I recalled more of the attack.

Safe now in southern Tasmania, I found it difficult to process these feelings in the context of the news of a man's arrest for violent crimes far away on the mainland.

The course of bringing that man to trial became a never-ending, permanent thread intricately woven into the background fabric of my life – ever present, sometimes surreal, always stressful.

It's over now. Bradley Robert Edwards has been found guilty of murder. There will, no doubt, be more to his story that will eventually be told.

This is my story, about what happened to me.

Trauma

1

I live in an exceptionally beautiful and peaceful part of the world: Hobart, Australia's southernmost capital. Drawn to the cooler climate and the slower pace of life, my husband Tim and I moved here from Western Australia in 2004.

Hobart reminds me in many ways of Perth forty years ago. You often meet people you know in the city, there are few security screens on doors and windows, and people are generally friendly, happy to stop what they're doing and chat for a while. Some people think Tasmania is a place that has been left behind, but that is precisely why I like it. The houses, especially in the city, are old and crooked, and you can sense the history, feel the presence of others before you. As you walk along the Hobart rivulet, past the historic Female Factory, certain spots send chills down your back and you just know that bad things have happened there in the past. But not now. I feel very safe walking the dog there. I know they're only memories of long ago, memories held by the land.

I was born in England, migrating to Western Australia with my parents and younger brother John when I was eleven years old. We were 'ten-pound Poms' – a small family hoping for a better life than postwar working-class England was offering, and we arrived in Fremantle with a great sense of excitement and anticipation. We lived at first in Bayswater with my dad's sister, who was our sponsor, until my dad secured a job in the industrial hub of Kwinana and we were allocated a Housing Commission house in the nearby southern suburb of Medina.

After finishing high school I did a short stint at Claremont Teachers College. In those days the main career options for girls were considered to be teaching and nursing. No-one from my cohort went on to university upon leaving school, although some, like me, did embark on tertiary education later, in their twenties or thirties.

I met my first husband, Matt, at a pub in Kalgoorlie when I was so very young – just twenty. He was Irish. He looked like a god, and he sang like a bird, but unfortunately, he also became violent when he drank too much alcohol, which was frequently. During most of the time I was with Matt, we lived in New Zealand. Looking back, it was only with the support of family in Australia and New Zealand that I managed to escape that relationship with what could be considered minor injuries: a cracked rib, bruised shins, a bloody lip. It was, of course, domestic violence, but nobody talked about that much in those days and I didn't make too much of a fuss about it. After we separated, Matt moved to South Africa to become a mercenary. I've sometimes wondered what happened to him after that.

Still young, and eager to see more of the world, I abandoned my teaching studies and travelled extensively, eventually finding myself in Germany where I met the man who would become my second husband – Dave, a military policeman in the British Army. After leaving the British Army, Dave joined the United Nations, and while he was serving in Israel we got married in Cyprus. We moved to Australia when I became pregnant with our first child: I wanted my family around me, and Dave planned to join the police force. Sadly, however, my mum died shortly after the birth of my first child, a daughter. I raised three baby daughters who were born in quick succession, and I supported Dave while he established his career in the Western Australia Police Force. Once my youngest daughter was well out of nappies, I began tertiary studies in social sciences at Curtin University, with a view to an eventual career in social work. In 1989, some two weeks after the whole family had travelled to Dubbo in New South Wales to spend a holiday with my brother John and his family, my dad had a massive heart attack and died.

After many years spent juggling parenthood, study and careers, Dave and I eventually separated in 1996.

I have now been married to my husband Tim for twenty years. We first met in 1988, when we were both mature-age students at Curtin University. We became good friends first, then work colleagues. We supported each other through painful relationship breakdowns, and we eventually built a life together. Tim has multiple sclerosis (MS), but despite this awful affliction he has become the mainstay, the rock of our family. For the past two decades he has been there for us all through a number of life traumas – always available, always calm, loving and supportive, no matter what's happening. Although painful, watching his physical decline, his terrible fatigue, has in some way given me greater perspective on life, a better capacity to manage my own trials and tribulations. He is the strongest person I know.

It is, for us, a peaceful, quiet and mostly predictable retirement, and I very much appreciate the change of pace that this time of life has brought. We live in a renovated old worker's cottage within walking distance of all that old Hobart Town has to offer. When we purchased the property it was very dilapidated, and we like to think we have saved it from decay and ruin. We let out a self-contained bedroom to guests, and people from all over the world have stayed with us, appreciated our location, the restaurants and facilities close by. My days now consist of slow lazy mornings, long easy walks with our dog, Maisie, a little gardening, shopping or cleaning in preparation for our guests, Pilates classes, occasional coffees with friends or my daughter Martha, who lives nearby with her family, grandchild-minding as needed, and a glass of wine before dinner. There are monthly visits to the cinema with my friend Lucy, a time for chatting and relaxing over good food followed by the latest movie. I love to read, to curl up in a warm, quiet spot for hours at a time, something I have done since I was a child. Twenty years ago I started creating mosaics, and I find this hobby meditative, relaxing, something to immerse myself in during the long winter months. It also produces something tangible to give to friends and family to express my gratitude and my love.

I have three daughters and four beautiful granddaughters – one here in Hobart, two in Perth and one in Darwin. My brother John lives in

New South Wales, and Tim's two sisters live in Western Australia. We have friends in Queensland and Western Australia and they have all, over the years, come to visit us in Hobart. Although Tim now rarely leaves the state, I travel to Perth nearly every year to catch up with friends as well as family, and to maintain old established connections that have sustained me through the years. Tim and I often travel together around Tasmania, exploring coastal hideaways and inland towns.

We live close to the river, the dog beach is at the end of our street, and there is a big playground with swings and slides just a few hundred metres down the road. It's a great spot for the grandchildren. Over the years I have pushed my grandbabies around this neighbourhood in their prams, Maisie trotting alongside, happy to be included in any activity. As the children got older we would walk slowly down the street towards the park, little fingers grasping my hand and Maisie straining on her lead, desperate for the pace to increase. Walking back usually involved stopping at every garden to pick a single flower to make a bunch to take home for their mums.

Christmas for us is a special family time, and everybody makes an effort to gather together every few years for the occasion. Because Tim finds travel so difficult these days, we usually host the celebrations, with everyone squeezing into our little house for Christmas lunch. Each person contributes something and the day generally passes without a hitch, the kitchen bustling with eager helping hands preparing and distributing delicious delicacies. We eat and talk and drink and laugh as we re-establish and strengthen our connections, watch the children play, and see how we've all changed since last we met together. I cannot imagine a finer celebration.

2

It was a week before Christmas in 2016 when, midway through icing the Christmas cake, I answered a call on our landline. The caller asked if I was Wendy Davis. I replied that I was, and she introduced herself as Katy, a detective senior constable from the Western Australia Police Force.

I was surprised, as I'd had no contact with WA police since my former husband Dave, who'd been a member of the force, had died in 2000 and I'd attended his funeral.

Katy went on to say that her team was investigating some possible links between a number of old crimes, and asked if I remembered any details about the assault that had happened to me some twenty-five years earlier, when I was working at Hollywood Repatriation Hospital in suburban Perth in 1990.

I was taken aback. I had not consciously thought about the attack for many years.

Katy asked me if I could run her through what I remembered and, oddly, once I'd started I couldn't stop. I remembered some details very clearly, while others came rushing back to me as I spoke. Every now and then she asked a specific question to clarify something. She was obviously taking notes.

As I spoke, a feeling of anger slowly engulfed me, and I told her this was the first time anyone had really listened to my account of the attack. I told her that, when it happened, I'd thought I was going to die, and nobody had seemed to understand, that no-one had listened to what I'd had to say. I told her I'd been astounded at the time that my attacker had only been charged with common assault. She didn't seem surprised at any of this, which puzzled me somewhat.

Other feelings were now also surfacing within me, including a sense of unease. For some reason I wondered whether she really was in the police force, and I asked her how she had located me given that I had changed my name and completely relocated a number of times since 1990. She laughed somewhat grimly and said: 'We have ways and means, and access to your driver's licence records.' It registered then that she must really have wanted to speak to me, and I became very curious and increasingly anxious. Had my attacker committed another crime after all these years? Could there have been other attacks at the time that they were only now linking to mine?

Katy asked me specifically whether I had seen my attacker's face. I felt sick and replied that no, I had not seen his face. At the end of our conversation she said she would be in touch again, and asked me to note down anything else I remembered about the attack in the meantime, and not to discuss our conversation with anyone as the investigation was continuing.

Tim had been listening to my side of the call, and as I put the phone down, I turned to him, puzzled. I relayed as much of the conversation to him as I could remember, and then we both stood looking at each other, unsure of what to think.

The evening passed with a slight sense of unreality. As well as discussing what could possibly have happened that this matter would resurface after twenty-five years, I began experiencing flashbacks of the attack. More details, strong surges of emotion – memories and feelings that I had buried for so long were starting to push their way to the surface, and that night I found it impossible to sleep.

Over the next few days I was consumed with preparations for Christmas. There was last-minute shopping to be done and, because my youngest daughter was trying to complete a PhD with a six-month-old baby, I was also doing a lot of childminding. In the midst of all this bustle and busyness, I kept remembering other details of the attack, but I tried to brush these memories and the now surging emotions aside as I carried on being a capable wife, mother and grandmother.

Part of me, though, had begun reliving that experience of twenty-five years earlier, and this was accompanied by an increasing sense of unease.

Katy's call had invoked much self-reflection. Even before I understood what was happening, I found myself looking back, anchoring myself in my history, and sensing that the world as I knew it was about to change.

3

Six days after that unexpected phone call – two days before Christmas – I awoke to the sound of my alarm, already planning out my busy day, which involved trying to avoid the Christmas rush at the shops and in the traffic. First up was Pilates. My usual class companion, my friend Vikki, was already celebrating Christmas with her family, so it would just be me that morning. I parked the car and turned off my phone: this was my time.

I hadn't slept well since the call from Katy, and I was very tired. Nat, my Pilates teacher, gave me an easy session, but I still had trouble concentrating on the exercises. There were preparations for Christmas dinner to consider, last-minute presents to be bought and, try as I might to forget it, my mind kept drifting back to the attack all those years ago. Halfway through the class, I suddenly remembered struggling and wriggling round to face my attacker; this memory kept replaying over and over in my mind, but I still couldn't remember what he looked like.

'Are you okay?' Nat asked, and I apologised and said my mind was elsewhere. I felt relieved when the class was over.

I walked slowly back up the hill to my car, got in and turned my phone back on. There were eight missed calls from home and two from a number I didn't recognise. My first thought was that something had happened to Tim. Over the years he has had many falls and several injuries related to 'bad MS days', and it is always with some trepidation that I leave him alone. Something was wrong.

I dialled home, and found that Tim was waiting: 'You need to ring Katy from the WA police,' he said immediately. 'It's urgent. I gave her your mobile number.'

Grateful that Tim was okay but with an increasing sense of apprehension, I called the other missed number. Katy answered immediately; she was waiting for my call.

'Wendy,' she said, 'we needed to contact you as soon as possible because there have been some developments in the case we've been investigating, and there will be a televised announcement later this morning. We wanted to speak with you so that you can prepare yourself. We have just arrested a man in connection with two of the Claremont serial killings that occurred in WA in the mid-nineties. His name is Bradley Robert Edwards, and he is the same man who attacked you in nineteen ninety.'

I felt a hollow, sick sensation in the pit of my stomach. The traffic noise surrounding me faded into the background, and everything outside the car became a blur.

Katy went on to say that she was sorry, that this must be a shock to me, that if I needed any help to deal with it I should let her know, and that I should continue to note down anything else I remembered about the attack. Her words echoed around in my mind, but I was still trying to process what she'd told me. All I could get out was, 'Thanks for letting me know.' She said she would leave me in peace to enjoy Christmas with my family, and would be in touch again in the new year.

My hands on the steering wheel, I sat motionless for some minutes. Then, stunned, I called home. When Tim answered I could barely get the words out: 'You need to make sure the news is on. The man who attacked me all those years ago has been arrested for two of the Claremont serial killings.'

I knew that Tim, like me, would be only too aware of the significance of the arrest. The 'Claremont serial killings', as they had become known, had been headline news in Perth throughout the mid-1990s, with the separate disappearances of three young women from the trendy nightlife strip in the affluent western Perth suburb of Claremont, and the subsequent discovery of two bodies. The body of the first woman to disappear has never been found.

'I knew it had to be something important for the police to contact you after all these years,' Tim replied. 'Are you okay to drive?'

I said I was. It did not occur to me that I might not be able to focus enough to drive safely. I did not consider that I might be engulfed by such strong emotions that I might not, in fact, be okay to drive. I started the car and headed home along my usual route, fortunately making it there without injury to myself or anyone else. I realised only afterwards that my mind did not register that drive at all – it was blank, and I was operating on automatic pilot.

Getting out of the car, I unlocked the front gate and looked around the garden, which suddenly seemed unfamiliar to me. Eager as always to welcome me home, my dog Maisie jumped up, and I patted her abstractedly before pushing her away. Tim opened the back door and we just stood there, staring at each other.

4

In May 1990 I was Wendy Randall, a forty-year-old social worker working in a senior position as a grief counsellor in the palliative care unit of the Hollywood Repatriation Hospital in the western Perth suburb of Nedlands. My husband, Dave, was working and studying hard to further his career in the Western Australia Police Force. We had two teenage daughters, Kate and Martha, with a third, Jo, just a year behind them.

My days were filled with the demands of work, both paid and at home, driving to and from work daily from the outer southern Perth suburb of Kelmscott, running the girls around to music lessons, sporting activities, part-time jobs and school events, and exercising our two large Rottweilers, Flossie and Cobber, who were very much part of our family. Every Thursday evening I piled the rotties into the car and drove Kate to the nearby suburb of Huntingdale where she had a guitar lesson. While she made music, I pounded the pavements with the dogs, taking the opportunity to provide both them and me with our daily exercise. I valued this rare quiet time alone.

I was full of energy, in the prime of my life, and every day brought new challenges to overcome and new experiences to enjoy. My friend Sheila had just had a baby boy, and I had been privileged to be her birth partner – the first person to hold the squealing, wriggling bundle of energy before he was whisked away to a humidicrib. They came straight to our house for the first few days after hospital, my girls fussing over the new baby while Sheila recovered from the birth and began learning how to be a mother.

My position in the palliative care unit was my second at the hospital. My first had been in the psychiatric unit, where I'd completed a sixteen-week placement during my final year of study at Curtin University some two years earlier. On gaining the position in palliative care, I'd undertaken further full-time study in death and dying as well as part-time study in family therapy. The hospital, recognising my interest and potential, had sponsored this study to assist in the development of my skills in working with terminally ill people and their families.

I worked with a very dedicated team of doctors, nurses and allied health professionals who specialised in end-of-life physical, emotional and spiritual care. My own role focused on grief and family counselling, and I worked with war service veterans of all ages and their families. Some people were in hospital for respite or pain management, while others were in the final days of their lives. My colleagues and I occasionally did home visits, and my job also involved an element of staff support. It was intense work, nursing the dying. Overall, it was demanding, often sad, but richly rewarding work that required patience and resilience and a strong respect for human life no matter how fragile. The ward environment was usually quiet and peaceful, with an emphasis on comfort and calm, pleasant surroundings. Staff trod quietly and spoke with low voices, and the general environment felt calm and safe.

At the time I was working there, Hollywood Hospital was undergoing some maintenance and upgrading its electrical and telephone systems. The automated telephone switchboard system for the part of the hospital where I worked was situated at the end of the palliative care ward. Work was ongoing, and there were often tradesmen and technicians around, easily identifiable by their hard hats, work overalls and identification badges. Security on the wards at that time was minimal, confined to an occasional reminder to lock up your valuables. There were no such things as mobile phones or laptop computers to worry about.

All my note-taking and report-writing was done by hand, sometimes at the nurses' station but more often in the quiet allied health office, an annexe-like structure that connected the back of the palliative care ward to a utility room and a toilet. I shared the allied health office with a senior occupational therapist and a senior physiotherapist but, because my colleagues sometimes worked on other wards, I was often alone in the office, and I used this time to make telephone calls, write up my notes and reports, and sometimes read books or articles relevant to my role.

The utility room was very occasionally used for meetings or as a private work area, because it was so quiet, and both it and the toilet could be locked from the inside. To get to the utility room from the ward, it was necessary to walk through the allied health office.

The allied health office was a smallish space, with room for three adjacent desks that looked out the office windows over a grassed area. My colleagues and I sat in wheeled, swivelling office chairs with our backs to the doors leading to the ward and the utility room. My desk was furthest from the ward, and closest to the utility room.

Although it was a bit out of the way, some of the nursing staff, doctors and orderlies occasionally used the toilet off the utility room behind us. If we were very busy and they were very quiet, they could sometimes pass behind us without our hearing – we didn't realise someone had gone to the toilet until we heard it flush!

I loved my work, and through it I established friendships that at the time I believed would endure for many years. I could feel myself growing in confidence as a practitioner as my skills and experience developed, and I was sure I had found my vocation.

5

After Katy's call and my drive home from Pilates that day in December 2016, I felt slightly sick and somewhat dissociated. The familiar sounds around me – the sparrows and blackbirds singing, the neighbours' dog barking, the soft hum of traffic from the main road – all seemed muffled and far away.

Tim and I watched the televised announcement by Western Australian police commissioner, Karl O'Callaghan. O'Callaghan had been at the police academy with Dave all those years ago, and it was strange seeing him standing there soberly talking about how police had made a significant breakthrough in the Claremont serial killings – crimes that had shocked the Western Australian community and led to the state's biggest and most complex investigation to date. O'Callaghan announced that in 2015 the Special Crime Squad had been allocated extra resources to investigate the killings as well as other offences that had occurred in the area at around the same time. As a result, a forty-eight-year-old Kewdale man had now been charged with the wilful murders of twenty-three-year-old Jane Rimmer and twenty-seven-year-old Ciara Glennon, who had disappeared from Claremont in 1996 and 1997, the abduction and rape of a seventeen-year-old woman in Claremont in 1995, and the sexual assault of an eighteen-year-old woman in Huntingdale in 1988, with both of the latter offences including deprivation of liberty. O'Callaghan went on to say that police were still investigating the 1996 disappearance of another woman from Claremont, eighteen-year-old Sarah Spiers. At the end of the announcement he emphasised the need to respect the privacy of the victims and their families as well as the judicial process that was now underway.

As we listened, I wondered whether O'Callaghan knew about the link with the ex wife of his old classmate. And was he wondering, like me, how Bradley Robert Edwards had managed to slip under the radar, given his arrest in 1990 for a violent unprovoked daylight assault on a lone woman committed while he was at work?

As the news started to sink in, there were so many questions swirling around in my head. Was this true? Had they really caught the Claremont serial killer after all these years? Did this mean I *had* been fighting for my life all those years ago? Why wouldn't anyone listen to me at the time? Why hadn't the attack on me been taken more seriously? Could he have been stopped from his brutal escalation if it had been? Was any of this my fault? Was I in some way responsible for those women's deaths?

I started to cry. Arms outstretched, Tim moved towards me. He held me until I became calm, and then we talked about what was happening. I felt completely traumatised by the long-buried emotions that were now resurfacing in the context of this new and horrifying information. We agreed that I needed to access some counselling to help me process what was happening.

As the day went on, the flashbacks I'd started having intensified. I could feel the sense of paralysis that had engulfed me as the cloth had muffled my screams. Big, strong fingers grasping my face, my neck, my body. The chair-back pressing into my spine. The surges of adrenaline as I struggled frantically to break his grip, and then the odd conflicting feelings of relief, fear and confusion as his grip suddenly loosened and I fell back and we stared at each other, him apologising over and over. The thought occurred to me then that I must have seen his face. How could I not remember what he looked like?

As I struggled to process all I'd heard that morning, I suddenly recalled the feeling of my face being squashed roughly against his chest, unable to move anything except my legs. I remembered that he was considerably taller and bigger than me. I also remembered the confusion of those around me straight after the attack, everyone trying to make sense of what had happened, how I'd escaped, and why this large, young man was left agitated, seemingly confused, upset and nearly weeping in the aftermath.

* * *

I went about the rest of that day doing the things that needed to be done to prepare our house for the impending Christmas celebrations. I tidied and cleaned, put some decorations up for the children, walked the dog, checked my list of last-minute preparations for the next day, Christmas Eve – pick up prawns, make cheesecake, defrost turkey roll, wrap the final presents, buy alcohol – all the while moving constantly between the present and the past, one minute coping and the next feeling tearful, anxious and increasingly angry.

By that afternoon, I was remembering other things that had happened in the days and weeks after the attack: references to Edwards' 'relationship problems' that had caused his supposedly 'out of character' behaviour; contact with Telecom (now Telstra) management, who had supported him, who had referred to the attack as an 'incident', who had seemed unable to understand its violence and had been more worried about its effect on his career than on my well-being; my feelings of powerlessness and disappointment at the lack of investigation and at the subsequent minor charge; and, underlying all this, my fear that he would come after me again.

Dinner preparations underway, I sat down with a glass of wine and, hoping for a distraction, scrolled through my social media feed. There he was! *Breaking news from Perth: Man arrested in relation to the Claremont serial killings.* It was him! The fear, the terror, surged through me as his face loomed up from the screen. Of course I had seen him! It was the same man. Older and larger, but the same man, with the same thick wavy hair, the same piercing, liquid dark eyes.

In the weeks and months after the attack, in order to sleep, to function at work, and in a desperate bid to return to 'normal', I had successfully blotted his face from my memory. But now, twenty-five years later, here he was. Heavier, older, greyer, but the same, looking up from my phone, at me, through me, staring, challenging me to deal with it again, to remember, this time in the context of violent abduction, rape and murder.

6

The attack occurred at my place of work in the early afternoon of 7 May 1990. It was my youngest daughter's eleventh birthday, and we had a family dinner planned at home that evening to celebrate, ahead of a party for her friends at the weekend.

I had been alone in the office for a while, working on a report, focusing on my writing. It was noticeably quiet, that post-lunch sleepy time when many of the patients were having a nap and nursing staff were at the nurses' station at the other end of the ward, preparing for the afternoon rounds. My colleagues were not around – perhaps they were on a home visit, maybe on another ward or even absent for the day. To me, it was just like any other day.

Apart from my long black cardigan, I don't remember what clothes I was wearing that day – a black skirt, probably, and a plain shirt; my 'work clothes' – or how I'd styled my hair. I do, however, remember my shoes. They were my favourites: a deep maroon colour with little narrow heels and a beautifully embroidered pink-and-red flower on the front. I wore them everywhere I could, despite the fact that they were a fraction too tight!

I was just working.

I had no inkling or premonition that what would happen to me in the next minutes would influence my life not once but again many years later as well.

The silence was broken by a slight sound from the direction of the door leading to the ward. I half-turned and glanced in that direction and, as I did so, a male voice asked: 'Is it okay to use the toilet?'

Caught up in my work, I registered that the voice's owner was tall and dark-haired, with clothes that identified him as a Telecom worker, one of many workers who had been around the hospital for what seemed like weeks. Nothing about his appearance or his manner indicated that anything was amiss. Eager to finish work early so I could get home to prepare the birthday dinner, I merely smiled, grunted and nodded, remaining focused on my work as he moved behind me towards the utility room and I swivelled back in my chair and resumed writing.

A few seconds later I heard the toilet flush, and I sensed him moving behind me again and walking back towards the ward door. But before my focus could fully return to my work, he stepped back into the office, saying, 'I dropped my pencil in the toilet – can I go and get it?'

As he moved behind me again, back towards the utility room, I thought that it was a strange request. It also registered in my brain that the toilet had flushed only seconds after he'd passed behind me the first time – too fast for him to have used it.

Before I could fully process these thoughts, I felt my head snap suddenly backwards over the top of the chair, as an outstretched hand holding a cloth came from behind and clamped over my mouth. An arm enveloped me roughly from the other side, pulling me backwards and upwards on my chair.

A deep, disappointed, sinking feeling flashed through me before I froze. It was a feeling so primal, a feeling of not being ready. I was petrified. I was sure there was something on the cloth to render me unconscious, and I was sure I was going to die. My heart nearly jumped right out of my chest, I was so afraid. I was completely paralysed. I was holding my breath to avoid breathing in whatever was on the cloth.

The arm tightened and I was being pulled further back, still on my chair, towards the utility room. My legs kicked out. I was desperately trying to fight against the force, to get a foothold on the carpet to anchor myself. My neck hurt and I couldn't hold my breath any longer, so I tried to breathe in. I could feel both cloth and hand pressed hard against my mouth and nostrils, against my teeth. My arms were pinned to my sides, completely bound by an arm holding me tight against the chair-back. The chair kept lifting off the floor.

Choking on the cloth, I suddenly realised that I hadn't passed out, that I had a chance, and my survival instinct kicked in. I started to really struggle. His arm tightened even more around my body and he tried to push the cloth further into my mouth, twisting my head as he pulled me harder towards the door. I could hear his breathing: heavy, fast. I struggled harder. As I managed to wriggle around, I was pulled off the chair, it clattered over and I could feel his fingers around my neck and the cloth being dragged from my mouth as my face was turned and pressed tightly against his chest.

Face now pressed tight against his chest, I was still being pulled towards the utility room. I couldn't move my arms, but I kicked him once in the shins with my left foot as hard as I could. The cloth was gone but still I couldn't scream, as my face was muffled against his chest. It was the longest ten seconds I have ever known, and I was sure I was fighting for my life.

And then suddenly, without warning or words, his grip loosened. I fell backwards and looked directly at him. He was just standing there, silent. I saw a lost, blank look in his dark, molten eyes. It was at once direct and terrifying. He was looking at me but at the same time through and beyond me as well. Was he *crying*? My brain was unable to register what had happened and, for just a moment, I had no idea what to do next.

As I carefully backed away, I kept my gaze fixed on his, ready for the first sign of movement towards me. I became aware that one of my shoes was missing and my clothes were in disarray, my cardigan half off.

He began to move slowly towards me, repeatedly mumbling, 'I'm sorry, I'm sorry, I'm sorry.'

In deep shock, but sensing that I was still at risk, I scrambled through the door to the ward and ran towards the nurses' station. Our Irish locum doctor, Hugh, had just emerged from one of the patient's rooms and, although I could barely speak, I managed to convey to him that I had been attacked. He went with a nurse to confront the attacker as I continued to run, stumbling through the ward to the nurses' station, where they called hospital security.

I remember little about the next few hours. I think the hospital security officer went straight to my office. I do not remember talking to him.

I felt spaced out. Nurses and other staff came in and out of the nurses' station. Someone brought me my missing shoe. I was given hot tea with brandy in it – 'for the shock', they said.

Everyone kept asking me what had happened, and I found it impossible to clearly articulate. I was terrified, shaking, full of disbelief about what had just happened. The police were called, and I was vaguely aware of two officers attending. I tried to explain what had occurred, but nobody seemed to understand.

Someone said that my assailant was just standing in my office, looking dazed. Someone said he had cable ties in his pocket; someone else said he was holding the cable ties in his hand. Someone said he was crying. Everyone seemed baffled; they didn't know what to say to me.

I was asked whether I had spoken to him before 'the incident'. Did I know him? Had I chatted with him? Made eye contact? Had I been friendly towards him? Smiled at him? I didn't know what to say. Had I smiled? I wasn't sure. They asked me how long the attack had lasted. I told them I didn't know; it had seemed a long struggle to me. They said maybe it had seemed like that, but it was just a few seconds probably.

Someone asked me, 'How on earth did you get away? He's much bigger than you!' I didn't know. My neck was hurting and my throat was sore. Nobody suggested I should have a medical assessment and I just wanted to go home. They said I was in shock and couldn't drive, and someone called Dave to come and get me. When he arrived and asked me what had happened, I couldn't verbalise it clearly. I was too traumatised. I seemed to have lost my voice. He was puzzled, and annoyed that he would have to leave his motorbike in the hospital car park so he could drive me home in my car. But he knew I never usually made a fuss about anything, and his expression was grim, worried. I don't know whether he spoke to anyone else at the hospital.

I don't remember the drive home. And I have no idea whether we celebrated my daughter's birthday that night.

7

Christmas Eve 2016 passed in a daze. On December 23, Bradley Edwards had appeared in the Perth Magistrates Court, smiling briefly, as the murder charges were laid against him. He was told he would be at liberty to apply for bail at some later stage, and no effort was made to suppress his identity.

I went through that day, and the next, as if on remote control. I collected the prawns, made the cheesecake, defrosted and cooked the turkey roll, wrapped the presents and bought the alcohol, all in a kind of trance.

I sent an email to Katy telling her that I had in fact seen my attacker, that I was struggling with my emotions and that I needed some help. Her response was immediate, and she promised to liaise with the Victims of Crime team in Perth to organise some counselling for me.

That night I drank more wine than usual and slept heavily but fitfully, waking at around three am, weeping and disoriented. I eventually drifted back to sleep, and when I awoke again it was Christmas morning. I had a heavy head and I was not sure I would make it through the day.

When the family arrived, and then our friends, I greeted them all with hugs but the gestures were automatic. Everything had assumed a dreamlike quality, and I felt totally dissociated from what was happening around me.

As I watched my three-year-old granddaughter opening her presents, I could see that she was understanding the act of giving and receiving for the very first time, but I was not able to appreciate it. I held my daughter's eight-month-old baby, but could feel no connection to this squirming little bundle of energy, normally a joy of my life.

I was fighting an unfinished battle, continually falling back into the shocked state I had experienced all those years ago, trying to contain my surging emotions. At times during the day I found myself without words; at other times my voice sounded too fast, too loud, and speaking was a major effort. I was sure my family and friends could tell that something was wrong with me.

As we started to eat, and without thought, I blurted out my news to the rest of the gathering. I told my daughters and our friends that someone had been arrested in Perth for the Claremont serial killings, and that he was, in fact, the same man who had attacked me at work in 1990. There was stunned silence. One friend had concern in her eyes; someone else seemed shocked and almost disbelieving.

Later that day I received a Christmas phone call from my brother, who now lives in northern New South Wales. The conversation began with the usual Christmas banter, but I could tell he was concerned about my unusually flat affect. When he asked, 'Is there anything wrong? You don't sound right,' it came bursting out: 'I've had some contact with the West Australian police force. Twenty-five years ago I was attacked at work, and the man responsible has now been arrested for the Claremont serial killings.'

'What?!' he said. 'When did this happen? Why didn't we know about it? Are you alright? What happened?'

That conversation would be repeated with other loved ones throughout that Christmas Day and the days that followed. The more I told the story, the more real it once again became and, although exhausted, I started to feel a little of the validation that had been missing all those years ago. It *had* been a violent attack. I *had* been fighting for my life, and I was lucky to be here now, telling the story.

My daughters were astounded. They all remembered the attack, and the fact that their normally very stable mother had been stressed, frightened and very, very angry. The anger was what they remembered most.

My eldest daughter, Kate, still lives in Western Australia. She was fourteen years old at the time of the attack, but she told me on that Christmas Day in 2016 that she had never forgotten the impact it had had on our family, on me. Now busy with her postgraduate psychology research in the burns unit of Fiona Stanley Hospital, she told me that, because of my experience, she was hypervigilant regarding the credentials of anyone unfamiliar entering the ward. I was amazed at this information. I'd thought it had all been buried in the past.

My oldest and closest friends in Western Australia were also shocked. Sheila said: 'Why didn't I know?' At the time it had happened we had been close and had shared many things, and I'm sure I would ordinarily have told her. But she'd been on holidays in the UK with her new baby, and by the time they'd returned I'd been well into the process of sublimation: I'd just wanted to forget it, to move on with my life. Confused and shaken at this latest news, Sheila was not sure what to say.

As the days passed, I found myself wanting to tell everybody who cared about me what had happened to me all those years ago. I wanted everyone to know what I had experienced, that it had been terrifying, that I had had to fight to survive. And now, at last, when I spoke about it, people seemed ready to listen.

8

For days after the attack, everything around me seemed slightly out of focus, and I found it extremely difficult to attend to my usual activities. I was constantly reliving the experience and trying to make some sense out of what had happened to me.

Although he was a police officer, Dave had no idea how to support me. Preoccupied as always with his work – with crimes involving other people – he just wanted me to get better, for everything to go back to normal. But everything wasn't normal. I was agitated and frightened and I couldn't relax. I froze at his attempts to embrace me. I lay awake next to him at night, listening to his steady breathing, wondering whether I would ever sleep again.

Because I had family responsibilities, and because I'd been taught to 'soldier on', I tried at least to appear calm. I didn't want my daughters to see my fear, to feel my anxiety. I was the mother, the strong one, the one who coped with everything, the one who helped others to deal with their grief, their trauma, their concerns, both at work and at home.

My neck hurt, and I worried that I might have sustained a whiplash injury. So for the first time since we'd moved into the area, I went to a local doctor. Gently moving my head from side to side, he checked my neck, noting the red marks and bruising left by the fingers of my attacker. He gave me something to help me sleep.

Because everything seemed out of kilter, I felt unsafe driving, and I didn't go back to work for a couple of days. At home alone, I was totally preoccupied with the attack, reliving every second, trying to work out exactly what had happened, and why. Why me? Had I smiled at him, encouraged him in some way, made eye contact? Not consciously, I knew, but I am a friendly person. I was sure we hadn't spoken. Who was he? Who would do such a thing? Was he really a Telecom worker? What had he been planning to do after he'd dragged me into the utility room? Why had he stopped? Had he actually been crying? What were the cable ties for? Had he been planning to use them on me?

I realised that, if he had succeeded in dragging me into the utility room and then locked the door, I would have been completely trapped. Nobody would have come in – they would have assumed that the room (or the toilet) was occupied. No-one would have been able to hear me. Over and over and round and round in my mind the experience continued to dominate every thought. But I still cleaned the house and walked the dogs, did the dishes and the washing and made the dinner.

Worried that my assailant would find out where I lived, I was also preoccupied with locking all the doors and windows, and grateful for the two Rottweilers that shared our home. Dave, who by then had spoken to the police involved about the attack, tried to reassure me that it was unlikely the attacker would come looking for me. He told me he had been arrested, that the police were handling it. He said it seemed that it had been a random attack, that he had been having some relationship problems, he'd just snapped, got carried away, momentarily lost control of himself.

I was not convinced, and I couldn't understand why Dave wasn't more concerned.

We talked about what he would be charged with, and Dave thought at least aggravated assault, given the bruising; possibly attempted deprivation of liberty, given the cloth over my mouth.

I kept expecting the police to contact me to discuss the attack further, but nobody did, so I assumed they had enough information to deal with it.

I stopped talking to Dave about what had happened. He was busy. He thought I was getting better, getting over it, and I didn't want to be a bother. I didn't want to make a fuss.

9

The days following Christmas 2016 blurred into one another as I continued to process the news of Edwards' arrest. Part of me was grateful to be living so far away from the enormous impact the arrest was having on the Western Australian media. Friends and family told me that Edwards' face was everywhere on the TV and on social media in Perth, and that everyone was struggling to come to terms with the quiet killer who had been living unsuspected in their midst.

I spoke again with Katy, who told me that Edwards' friends and neighbours, sporting club members and work colleagues were all having trouble reconciling those terrible acts with the person they'd thought they knew.

Although I was happy to be relatively removed from the media frenzy, I also repeatedly searched for Edwards' name online to check for any updates and to continually reconfirm to myself that yes, it had happened, and there he was, the same man who had attacked me. I read every media report about him I could find. I wanted to try to understand his story, to understand just what had happened to me, and to those young women whom he was accused of murdering.

***

Bradley Robert Edwards was born in country Western Australia in 1968. The elder of two sons of Bruce and Elizabeth Edwards, he attended Huntingdale Primary School in south-eastern Perth and then neighbouring Gosnells High School, just a few years ahead of my daughters who went to nearby Kelmscott High. He joined Telecom in 1986, training to become a technician. In 1989 he began a relationship with the woman who would become his first wife, and they married in late 1991.

As I read this, I wondered whether she was the person with whom he'd been 'having relationship problems' in 1990 when he attacked me?

The couple lived in a house in Huntingdale until the mid-1990s, when they parted ways and subsequently sold the house. This was around the same time the Claremont killings began.

I speculated about what might have been happening to Edwards during this time. Was he having more 'relationship problems'? Did the marriage breakdown tip him over the edge?

After the house was sold, Edwards moved back in with his parents who lived nearby in the same suburb.

The police were now searching the Huntingdale house – in the suburb where I'd spent hours walking the Rottweilers while Kate had had her guitar lessons. Was the street where he had lived one of the streets I had walked? By some coincidence, could I even have passed him back then, perhaps nodded hello as I focused on controlling the dogs and thought about what I would be preparing for dinner?

Edwards met the woman who would become his second wife in 1997. The couple, along with the woman's daughter, purchased a fibro house in the Perth suburb of Kewdale in July 2000. When they separated in 2016, Edwards remained living at the property with his stepdaughter.

Detectives and forensic police were also searching the Kewdale house, as well as a house in Madora Bay, south of Perth, that had belonged to Edwards' parents in the 1990s.

Media reports said that Edwards' neighbours and acquaintances described him as 'quiet', 'amiable', 'a bit aloof'. He apparently liked computer games, and had occasionally helped neighbours out with computer issues. For many years he had been involved with the Kewdale Little Athletics Club, first with his stepdaughter and then in various key roles within the organisation. In recognition of their volunteer work, both Edwards and his wife had been made life members of the Belmont Little Athletics Centre. He had also received awards for his community service and been photographed with politicians. He was a West Coast Eagles fan. He had worked for Telstra (formerly Telecom) for more than thirty years. All in all, he had been living an apparently ordinary suburban life for decades.

In the weeks following Christmas 2016, more details began to emerge about the events that had led up to his arrest. It appeared that the task force assigned to the case had matched DNA found under Ciara Glennon's fingernails with DNA found on a kimono dropped at the scene of the sexual assault of an eighteen-year-old woman in Huntingdale in 1988. Edwards had been nineteen years old at that time – it was two years before he attacked me. I vaguely remember the press that had surrounded that attack – the photograph of the white kimono on the front page of the newspaper, and the speculation of a possible link with other articles of women's clothing that were being stolen from clotheslines at night in the area. The newspaper reports had served as a reminder to locals to secure their doors and windows; there was a prowler around. Reports also mentioned a DNA link with another assault in 1995, in which a seventeen-year-old woman had been abducted and raped in a cemetery as she'd been walking home. But apparently, neither of these earlier victims had seen their attacker. So how did the investigators know it was Bradley Edwards? There were some missing links, and I was becoming increasingly desperate to know the story as my own memories were starting to overwhelm me.

10

Sometime during the week following the attack, Dave and I were invited to attend a meeting with a representative from Telecom. My understanding was that this man was a senior manager, someone responsible for staff. The meeting was held in a large office in a building somewhere along Stirling Highway, in the suburb of Mosman Park, if I recall correctly. I am almost certain it was a police station: I have a memory of checking in at a desk when we arrived. I don't remember whether anyone else was present at the meeting, although I do have a vague memory of being led into the room and being seated by someone in uniform. I remember a beard, someone wearing shorts and long socks.

I was still in shock and very vulnerable, but I can remember quite clearly much of what was said during that meeting because it made me so terribly angry. I still feel angry now, writing about it.

Dave and I had talked in the car on the way to the meeting. Half joking, perhaps in an attempt to allay some of my anxiety, Dave had speculated that Telecom probably wanted to ensure that I wouldn't be suing them. Until then I had not even considered this as a potential outcome for them to manage. During the times I'd been able to think rationally about the attack, I just wanted the police to by some means ensure that my attacker wouldn't do it again, that he was punished appropriately as a deterrent, and that he would receive some help to control his behaviour in future. I also wondered why he'd done it, and whether he'd ever done anything like it before. There could be absolutely no excuse for his violent behaviour, I was sure about that. We were both sure he would lose his job.

The Telecom manager sat across the table from us, his arm sprawled across the tabletop. But his manner did not feel casual, it felt like authority, and there was tension in the air. He began by apologising on behalf of Telecom for the 'unfortunate incident' that I'd been involved in. Still fragile and trying to process what had happened, I felt myself bristling. Dave commented, 'This was not an "incident" – it was an attack, mate. He lost it.'

Someone enquired as to how I was coping now that things had settled down a bit, and whether I had sustained any injuries. I said I was still traumatised, that I had bruising on my neck, and I was not sleeping.

I was trying to work out what the purpose of the meeting was. I had already been told that because the police had been involved, my assailant would be charged – with what, exactly, I did not yet know. But the Telecom manager explained that 'young Bradley' had been having 'relationship problems'. I remember the words 'sensitive', 'fragile', 'completely out of character', 'a one-off incident'. He had, apparently, never done anything like this before. He was a 'good worker', with 'a good future ahead of him', he was sorry for what he'd done and he had agreed to get some counselling to help him manage his anger, deal with his emotions. The manager went on to say that, although he understood that I was shocked by what had happened, it would not benefit anyone if this promising employee lost his job, his career.

I was rendered speechless for a moment or two. When I recovered, I told him that I'd thought I was going to lose my *life*. I told him it was not normal behaviour to attack a complete stranger because you were having difficulties in your relationship. I said that he'd had cable ties in his pocket, that he'd put something over my mouth, tried to drag me into the toilet, that I was still bruised and in shock.

The manager told me that cable ties were part of standard Telecom equipment, that it would not be considered unusual for a technician to carry them while at work. He reiterated that the employee had never done anything like this before; he had been under a great deal of emotional pressure when the 'incident' had occurred, and counselling would help him to deal with his current personal issues. He said the employee was prepared to plead guilty to common assault, and there was really not enough evidence to charge him with anything more.

I couldn't believe what I was hearing. I tried to remain calm as I again attempted to explain that I had been terrified during the attack, that it had been totally unprovoked, that it had left me traumatised and that the behaviour was not a normal response to personal stress.

Other than nodding, the manager did not respond. He looked serious, and somewhat annoyed at me for making such a fuss. He was clearly not hearing my account of the events, and I felt increasingly unable to communicate the violence of the attack or my terror. I was close to tears, and I felt sick. I just wanted to go home.

I don't remember anything else about the meeting. I do remember feeling completely disempowered and increasingly anxious, concerned and angry as I waited to find out what would happen to my assailant.

11

In those days following Christmas 2016, I found it increasingly difficult to sleep. I felt exhausted and emotionally fragile. The anger that I'd felt back in 1990 – at my attacker, at Telecom, and at the WA police – was now resurfacing with a vengeance. I was also anxious much of the time. I burst into tears at the slightest provocation, and I felt overwhelmingly guilty about the young women who had been attacked in the years following the incident. My mind went round and round, trying desperately to think of things I could have done differently, to rationalise what had happened, to understand everything within this new context of brutal murder.

Katy informed me that she had made contact with the Victims of Crime service in Perth, and I received an email from them saying they'd referred me to their Hobart counterparts and I should expect a call from them in the new year.

Because the enormity of what was happening didn't affect those around me – nobody in Hobart had even heard of the Claremont serial killings – I avoided everyone except close family. The combination of anxiety, fear and anger was very unsettling, and flashbacks from the attack and its aftermath interrupted my daily routine as I remembered more details and tried to make sense of both what had happened and what was now happening.

A week or so into the new year, I saw a counsellor from the Victims of Crime service in Hobart. I talked, and she listened and clarified and validated, and gradually I gained some perspective and felt a little better able to cope. She suggested that journalling, or writing down all my thoughts and feelings, would be a good way to process the emotions that had begun to overwhelm me since Katy's first call. She told me that the process of bringing Edwards to trial would likely take many months, even years, that I would probably have to go to Perth to appear as a witness and, importantly, that the prosecution team would help to prepare me for my part in the trial.

This was the first time I'd considered the legal process that Edwards' recent arrest had initiated, and I felt a jolt of fear, of apprehension, for the part I might have to play in it. What if I didn't get it right? What if he got off again? But then the reality swept over me that he had been arrested for two murders and two other serious assaults, and that the police must have indisputable forensic evidence that would be used to convict him of these terrible crimes. It would all be okay. I would just have to tell my story. And this time they would listen.

12

I am normally a calm, rational person. It takes a lot to upset my equilibrium, to unsettle me. I rarely cry, I never become hysterical, I am generally able to cope with whatever is happening at any given time. I have a strong belief in my own ability to get on with things, to move forward, to deal with any setback that might arise. The attack at Hollywood Hospital engendered feelings in me that I had never previously felt: feelings of great terror, anxiety and fear. Those few brief seconds had a far worse impact on me than the domestic violence I had experienced in my first marriage. There had been no warning, no preparation for what I was about to experience. I was in shock for days afterwards, quiet and withdrawn, and I see now that this might well have been part of the difficulty I had in conveying the terror of my experience. Busy with his work, Dave assumed I was recovering. I did, after all, go back to work after a few days, so maybe it hadn't been so bad. Perhaps if I had completely lost it, someone might have understood how terrifyingly violent those few moments had been.

* * *

After our meeting with the Telecom manager, Dave and I heard nothing further from the police for a few days. Then one day, with both of us home at a reasonable hour for a change, Dave called them for an update. Our house was in the Kelmscott hills, on the side of an escarpment looking out across the plains below, towards the Indian

Ocean. Dave was standing by the dining room window gazing out at this view as he spoke on the phone. I was watching him and listening intently, trying to pick up the gist of the conversation.

'Thanks, mate,' Dave said finally. Putting the phone down, he turned to me and sighed heavily. 'He's been charged with common assault.'

'What does that mean?' I asked.

'Not much,' Dave replied. 'He's probably looking at a fine, or probation, maybe some anger-management counselling. They said they didn't have enough evidence to charge him with anything further.'

I started to cry. 'I thought there was something on the cloth!' I was soon sobbing, and then hyperventilating. 'I thought I was going to die – don't you understand? There was no-one else there! He had cable ties in his pocket! He could have raped me – he could have killed me! What if he does it again? What if he comes after me again?'

Dave was taken aback. This was not the reaction he'd been expecting. Disappointment, frustration, probably anger. But definitely not near-hysteria. Up until this point I had been quiet, withdrawn, sometimes tearful but attempting to appear calm, rational and stoic.

Dave said that he thought it was too late but he would speak to the police involved again to see whether the charge could be upgraded, maybe to aggravated assault, and whether they wanted to speak with me further. But by now I didn't believe that anything would change. It seemed as though the police and Telecom had closed ranks in support of my attacker, and I felt humiliated, disbelieved, powerless, disillusioned, alone, and very, very angry.

13

Katy had started drafting my police statement after that first phone call. As I recalled more details, we refined it. Towards the end of January 2017, she emailed me to say that she and a colleague, Brendan – a detective sergeant who had been my liaison person when Katy had taken leave earlier that month – would be flying over to Tasmania to spend a couple of days interviewing me and finalising the statement. She said she thought I would be likely to remember even more once she and Brendan spoke to me in person.

I was unsure how I felt about this. Given my experience with police twenty-five years earlier, I wondered if they would properly hear and understand me now.

Tim and I had planned a week away, mostly to relax and to give me an opportunity to digest what the last month had thrown in my direction. I told Katy I would be able to speak with them after our break, and she said she would organise their flights accordingly.

Feeling overwhelmed by the conflation of the past and the present, I had, for the past few weeks, been following the counsellor's suggestion and writing about what had happened and what I was experiencing now as events continued to unfold across the country. The house was littered with writing pads and scraps of paper filled with unrelated recollections that I'd jotted down as they'd surfaced. Now, in an attempt to regain some control over my fluctuating emotions, I decided to put them all together, and purchased a secondhand laptop for this purpose.

Tim and I went to a quiet riverside hamlet in Tasmania's south-east called Charlotte Cove. Our accommodation had floor-to-ceiling windows that looked out over a wide expanse of water, and I knew the moment I entered that it would be good for me.

Those first few days away were hard. Gradually, as I started to transcribe the notes I'd made into a logical sequence – a timeline – the story began to emerge. My anxiety levels were high as I detailed my experiences around the attack, the surging memories sometimes painful. As the week went on, the more I went over each memory, refining my account, remembering more details, something started to fall away and it got a little easier. It was finally coming out.

I found myself able to relax on long beach walks with Maisie, after which we sat, side-by-side on the couch, staring out at the water, both mesmerised by the shimmering view. Tim and I spoke little; he understood that this peace and quiet would refresh me and help me to prepare for the days and months ahead. I found myself less focused on searching for the latest updates on Bradley Edwards, and being so far away from Western Australia there was nothing in the local news about the arrest. I could feel myself starting to regain some perspective. As the week went on, it was almost as if I was writing about someone else. But I could not escape it completely.

Two days before we were due to return home, Katy sent me an email confirming that she and Brendan would be flying over the following week to spend some time with me going through my statement. She asked if I could locate any relevant photos of myself from the time of the attack, and I said I would look through the old albums when we got home. I told her I was looking forward to meeting them – but was I? Part of me was hoping that this would all go away so my life could return to normal – that is, the 'normal' that I'd felt when I'd thought I had been randomly, violently attacked by a now-remorseful man who'd had a temporary one-off lapse of control, not by a serial killer and rapist who, I now believed, had been refining his technique and who, for some reason, whether deliberate or accidental, had spared my life.

14

After just a few days at home following the attack, I'd returned to work. Only my immediate family and my colleagues knew about it. When other workmates enquired about what had happened and the aftermath, I remember puzzled looks and surprised expressions when I told them of the charge brought against my attacker. It seemed to me that, apart from a few close colleagues who recognised the impact the attack had had on me, those who observed the bruising around my neck and the friend who, shocked, referred to the 'attempted strangulation', nobody else seemed to be interested or concerned that my attacker had not been charged with anything more serious than common assault. When I mentioned it to Dave, he reiterated that there was not enough evidence to charge him with anything further. It seemed to me that everyone had accepted that my attacker was a good person who had 'snapped' under pressure, that he would never do it again, that he was not a danger to anyone else, that a few counselling sessions would fix things.

I felt sick and anxious and confused; I even doubted myself, my own experience. If there was more to it, surely the police would have charged him accordingly? Surely Telecom would have been more concerned? Perhaps it hadn't been as violent, as terrifying, as bizarre as I'd thought. It was as if the lesser charge had diminished the attack in everyone's eyes and, feeling totally negated, I stopped talking about what had happened. The attitude of the Telecom manager, the lack of police contact, the knowledge that my attacker was unlikely to be punished appropriately for the trauma he had caused me, the ongoing fear that he might come after me again, all contributed to my sense of despair. For me, the terror I'd experienced in those few minutes and the trauma of the ensuing days and weeks became something that no-one else understood.

Because I'd returned to work after just a few days and appeared to be coping, hospital management focused their attention on the occupational health and safety implications of the attack. I don't remember whether I was offered counselling. Perhaps not. I *was* a counsellor. There was a lot of discussion about the placement of alarms that could be activated in case of another 'emergency', a little red button on our desks that we could push if we were attacked.

I found myself distracted from my work, more concerned about my environment, unable to be alone in the office, uncomfortable with lone home visits. I was hypervigilant, overly aware of sound and of people's movements, always looking out for strangers on the ward, suspicious of visitors. My work suddenly became joyless and depressing.

I turned my attention to my family, and began to consider new employment. I applied for another job. I knew I would be leaving a secure permanent Commonwealth Government job for a lesser-paid position in the non-government sector, but I was unable to stay. Within two weeks of returning to work, I handed in my notice. Bitterly disappointed in 'the system', in the police, and in Telecom, I began to bury the attack deep in my mind. I didn't follow up to see what happened to my assailant, I forgot his name, his face gradually became a blur and I let my very busy life sweep me along and away from the whole thing.

Inside, though, I was devastated. I felt I had lost the work that I'd loved so much, the career that I'd just been establishing. I felt so guilty that the hospital, the palliative care unit and the social work department had invested so much in me in terms of extra knowledge and education, and now I was leaving.

What happened to me over those dreadful weeks also affected my relationship with Dave, and my trust in people in general. I felt totally unsupported, and as if I had in some way been 'managed' by the police force and by Telecom. When thoughts of the attack surfaced, as they did frequently during those first few weeks afterwards,

I wondered uneasily what was happening to my attacker. Would he be jailed? Would he be angry? Would he be looking for me? Why had he assaulted me? Would he do it again to some other unsuspecting victim? At the same time, I just wanted to bury it all, to pretend it hadn't happened. As I tried to suppress all my fear and anger, for the first time in my life I started to suffer from insomnia.

Over the next years, the next decades, in different places, different contexts, with different colleagues, different friends, thoughts of what had happened very occasionally flashed to the surface. Triggered perhaps by someone telling me of their telecommunications experience, or by a relative getting a job with Telecom (later Telstra), or even by seeing an advertisement or a logo, I would say, 'I was attacked by a Telecom worker at work.' People would reply, 'What did you do?' 'Why did he attack you?' 'Did you know him?' Someone once even asked me, 'What did you do to upset him?'

When they asked me, 'What happened to him?', I would say, 'He was charged with common assault,' and they would look at me and I could see they were thinking that it couldn't have been that bad, that I was doing okay, and I would let it sink back down again to where it was hidden from view.

15

It was the end the first week of February 2017 when I opened the door to the two detectives from Perth. I was anxious, unsettled, and unsure of what the day would bring. Katy and Brendan were friendly, respectful, and obviously aware that the meeting would not be easy for me. As the day progressed and we went over and over the attack, further details came back to mind.

They had clearly done their own research, and they informed me that I had resigned on 17 May 1990, just ten days after the attack. I remembered then that I had enquired about a new position soon after I'd returned to work. It was a job that I had previously declined an invitation to apply for, because I had been so happy in my role.

In our discussions, it became clear that the basic details of the attack had been very succinctly recorded and presented when Edwards had faced the charge in court some two weeks after the event. They showed me the police report, and it was like reading about something that had happened to someone else. It was brief, almost clinical. In no way did it reflect the terror I had experienced. There was no reference to the isolation of the office, to the fact that he had effectively held me captive for those long seconds until I had managed to break free, that he had, in fact, attempted to abduct me and drag me to a secluded area, that I had been injured and traumatised.

There was no signed statement from me. I don't remember making any report. Nobody had followed up with me regarding obtaining any further details that I might have been able to provide once the shock had worn off. No-one had come out to have another look to make sense of what had happened. No-one had been interested. I could feel my disappointment, my anger, my despair welling up inside me, raw again after all these years.

According to Brendan, even if my attacker had been charged with aggravated assault, the police had felt that there was not enough evidence for a charge of deprivation of liberty or any other more 'serious' crime. As the Telecom manager had suggested at our meeting, the cable ties could have been attributed to his work. They were unable to prove that he had intent; he had no previous record, there was an assumption that this was his first offence, and he maintained that he had just snapped. The fact that he had gagged me and pulled me backwards towards a secluded, lockable room seemed to have been overlooked.

I was trying to take in all the information the detectives were giving me, but thoughts of what had happened all those years ago kept getting in the way. I think Katy said that Edwards' then-girlfriend and/or his mother went to court with him and vouched for him, so that when he married that same woman a short time later, both she and his mother probably knew what he had done. He had received two years probation and been ordered to have a psychiatric assessment and psychological counselling. I wondered whether the assessment had given any indication of his violent inclinations, and what sort of counselling had been ordered. Had he attended? Had he shown any real remorse for his actions? Or had he thought I was small, alone, easy prey? Had his technique at that stage been still unrefined, his failed attack on me subsequently indicating that he needed to sedate or better restrain his future victims? Had that attack been part of his preparation for future atrocities? I had so many questions. But they were questions that the detectives couldn't answer.

During our discussions, Katy asked me to draw a diagram of the allied health office I'd been working in that day, showing its situation within the context of the ward and the wider hospital. It was very clear in my mind and, as I concentrated, I felt a resurgence of the general unease and trepidation that had persistently threatened me since that first phone call some six weeks earlier. Maisie lay under the table, close to me. She was not her usual friendly and excitable self. Picking up on my anxiety, she started to obsessively lick her feet, a sure sign something had upset our usual calm equilibrium.

I had unearthed two photographs for them to take back to headquarters. One was of me receiving my Certificate in Palliative Care, during the year before the attack. I am wearing my favourite shoes – the ones I was wearing on the day of the attack – and Dave is in the audience. The other, taken just weeks before the attack, was of me at a party with some nursing colleagues, one of whom was on duty the day of the attack and was first on the scene along with the locum doctor. In it, I am smiling, wine glass in hand, happy with my work and my life.

Before they left, the detectives shared some information about the identification of Edwards as a suspect in the Claremont killings. New DNA technology had helped the task force investigating the crimes to link crimes spanning nearly a decade, from 1988 to 1997. Armed with these links, they had broadened their search to other potentially related criminal incidents occurring in the Claremont area and surrounds during and around that time span. They were eventually able to match fingerprints from a 1988 incident in Huntingdale to fingerprints taken when he was charged with the attack on me.

It appeared that something positive had emerged from the trauma that I had experienced all those years ago. Together with advances in DNA technology, it eventually and somewhat belatedly had assisted in catching a serial killer.

All up, Katy and Brendan spent about eight hours with me over two days. It was exhausting but useful to them and to me. For them, the information that I provided would help to firm up the prosecution's case against Edwards. For me, it was cathartic to be able to talk about what had happened in those brief moments of terror, and to finally have my experience validated by the Western Australian police.

* * *

Two days later, after Katy and Brendan had returned to Perth, they visited Hollywood Hospital. Much had changed since 1990, but they were able to identify the scene from my diagram, and Katy told me that my recollections were accurate. The annexe area was still being used as an office and, when they entered the room, a worker was sitting, back to the door, in exactly the same position that I had been at the time of the attack. Katy said when she had seen them, she'd felt a chill run down her spine. Surveying the crime scene and recreating the events of the attack, it must have been obvious to them that Edwards was familiar with the environment, that he had planned the attack and that I was very lucky to have escaped relatively unharmed. I still don't understand why that wasn't apparent or taken into consideration at the time of the attack.

16

Over the five years following the attack, my life changed considerably. I left the hospital and obtained work in the disability sector. With a new job and new colleagues – with nobody to remind me of what had happened – I was eventually able to bury the events of the past. But I still felt their impacts. I felt less secure, my confidence was shaken, I was less trusting of those close to me, and I no longer had any faith in the police force or in the legal system in general.

Because I had invested so much of myself into that palliative care grief-counselling role, it took some time for me to adjust to a new working environment. Although my knowledge of death and dying and the grief process was still helpful, the people I was now working with were very much alive, and with very different issues. For three years I worked at Rocky Bay, a disability services provider in the Perth suburb of Mosman Park; I then moved to the Disability Services Commission, obtaining work with their new Local Area Coordination program. The early 1990s was a time of changing values and attitudes towards people with disabilities, and much of my time was spent supporting people to become more included in the community, advocating for them to have access to the same basic rights as the rest of society: respect, a home, education, employment, and relevant community services and supports. I eventually grew to love this work, and my life during this period was enriched both personally and professionally by the many and varied people I met in my new career.

My career advanced and I took on more responsibility, relishing in the activity and the sense of accomplishment.

During this time, I, like many of my colleagues in the 'helping professions', undertook further counselling and training to assist with my own personal development. The strength and knowledge that this personal work afforded me also further developed my professional skills, and I gained a great sense of contribution and value from my working roles. It also helped me to deal with my own changing personal relationships. My daughters were by now spending less time at home, and were all experimenting with their own relationships and how they fitted in to the world. Not once during this personally intense time, though, did I consciously consider the attack. It was well hidden in my subconscious, buried deeply along with all the emotions it had ignited.

During this same period, Dave and I undertook two trips together. The first was to Nepal, a country that I had visited in my own early travels. The second was to the Kimberley region in the north of Western Australia. Things happened on both of those trips that cemented our differences, and we grew further and further apart.

Our journey to Nepal was a huge joint adventure with my friend Kerry, a nurse from Rocky Bay, and her husband, Mike. Dave and I had previously been away together a few times on short weekend trips to the south-west of Western Australia, and each time we'd returned things had always been in order – dogs and cats fed, dogs exercised, the house neat and tidy and the girls happy and safe. But when we went away just for a weekend neither of us was totally relaxed, and we felt that perhaps spending more time together would help our relationship. For me, there was also huge excitement in returning to a place that I had explored during my youth. I could, for a short while, be a traveller and not just a mother and a worker, and I hoped the totally different environment would help Dave to leave work and study behind and we could just have some fun together. And so, having organised for friends to call in on the girls – who eagerly assured us that yes, they could manage without their parents for a couple of weeks – we left on our adventure.

I can remember some good things from that trip. That first sultry night in Singapore, as the four of us wandered around the markets, stopping at a small sidewalk stall to eat noodles and drink beer that became warm as soon as you poured it into a glass. Me wanting to stop and chat to every mangy, stray cat that crept out from under the small cars parked bumper to bumper along the narrow streets. Dave laughing loudly as he threw off his mantle of responsibility for the first time in so long. The excitement I felt as I looked out the aircraft window and saw flashing glimpses of the Kathmandu Valley between the clouds. The more Dave relaxed, the more his excitement grew, and I thought everything would be okay and we would enjoy the next couple of weeks.

But it wasn't all to be so easygoing. First up we joined an eleven-day trek around the foothills of Everest. There were about ten of us in the group, with a similar number of Nepalese porters who forged ahead carrying vast loads of camping equipment and supplies on their backs. I remember two young English women, teachers I think, another woman in her thirties, a nurse who struggled with the leeches that latched onto our calves as we crossed the streams and climbed higher and higher up the mountainside, and a young couple from New Zealand who were always half a day ahead of the rest of us. Dave nicknamed them 'the flying Akubras', because of their matching wide-brimmed hats. Our nightly campsites were surrounded by exquisite scenery, majestic towering peaks topped with snow. The thin mattresses and rocky ground were more than compensated for by the breathtaking views and by the friendly villagers we met every day. We slept the sleep of the physically exhausted every night, and were woken by steaming cups of tea outside our tent at dawn.

The highlight of the trek, some halfway through, was to be a night in a village high on the mountain, dining and partying with the locals, and we were all looking forward to the experience. Unfortunately, a few days before that night, I became quite unwell. For two days I struggled up and down the slopes with a knifing pain in my side, stopping every half-hour to relieve myself behind bushes, and becoming weaker and weaker. On the second evening, through my pain, I watched the face of the Nepalese tour guide darken with concern as he and Dave took one arm each and hauled me the last few hundred metres to the camping spot that had been prepared by the team. Earlier in the day the guide had examined me, conferred with the nurse in our group and given me antibiotics for a suspected kidney infection. I would miss the party, and we would all have a rest day the next day so that I would be fit enough to continue the trek. I could sense Dave's disappointment at missing out on all the fun at the village dinner, but I felt so unwell and I didn't want to be alone, so we settled ourselves in our tent and prepared to have a quiet night. As the evening wore on, we could hear people from the group laughing as they left one by one to join the villagers, then the sound of music ebbing and flowing as it travelled through the night air. I was lying and leaning on Dave as I was trying to rest, to doze off, when he shifted suddenly and unhooked himself from me. He moved away and asked if I would be okay if he joined the party. I could sleep, he said. There was no point in both of us missing out. Exhausted, I merely nodded. Hours later, he stumbled back in, drunk with excitement and local beer. I felt unsupported, abandoned, but I didn't say anything. I didn't want to make him angry, to spoil our trip, so I thought it was better not to make a fuss.

I was, by this time, becoming very aware that there was something missing in my relationship with Dave. The things that had attracted us to each other when we'd first met had changed – or perhaps it was that our view of them had altered, worn down by the avalanche of three small children, demanding jobs, mature-age studies and very hectic lives. When we'd met, he'd seen a strong, independent woman who had travelled halfway round the world by herself. He'd since watched me deal capably with the deaths of both my parents, the births of three children in rapid succession, and university study, all while managing a family. I think the attack at Hollywood Hospital was something of a turning point for both Dave and me in terms of our relationship. For the first time, he'd seen a very vulnerable side of me, a side that needed to be held, comforted, reassured, and he was not comfortable in that role. For my part, what I'd seen all those years ago as steadfast and stoic had, it seemed to me, become boring and grumpy; what had attracted me as quick and clever humour I now saw as sarcastic and evasive, a way of avoiding any deeper interaction. Neither of us recognised the insecurities buried deep within the other.

In addition, as the girls grew older and there was a little less daily responsibility, a little more space, I started to examine my own needs more closely, and I started to change. I read many books – books about women and personal growth, about spirituality and meditation, about oppression and freedom. Someone gave me a copy of Clarissa Pinkola Estés' *Women who Run with the Wolves*, and I devoured it hungrily, trying to find myself in its pages. I purchased scented oil and asked a bemused Dave to massage my feet, but he would not; he thought it was bizarre. The more I emerged, the more noise I made, the more I found my voice, the more he retreated. He plodded on, focusing on his work and his studies, steadfastly ignoring all the warning signs of an impending tsunami.

In mid-1995, we made what I now see was a final desperate attempt to stay together. We bought a secondhand Nissan Patrol four-wheel-drive with a camper trailer, loaded it up with supplies for three weeks, and headed north. It was a bumpy start, both of us a little concerned about leaving the girls. They were by now busy with study and part-time work, but they had lots of friends and we had fears that our house would become the local party house. After a night at the Meekatharra Hotel – with many reassurances from me to Dave that, when I'd worked there as an underage seventeen-year-old during my travels in 1967, there had been no topless barmaids – we walked out to a flat tyre on the Patrol. My heart sank – not because of the flat tyre, but because I knew that Dave would find it stressful, that he would become angry, and that our day would be ruined. And he did. And it was.

Although there were times during the next few weeks when we relaxed, when the peace and solitude of the Kimberley seeped into our bones and we were kind to each other, we couldn't quite make the deeper connection that we both wanted. An incident in Broome was, I think, the final nail in the coffin. In town for a meal, there was a couple seated near us. She was young, very attractive; he was older, our age. They had a young child. Dave couldn't take his eyes off them. He made some comment about it probably being a second marriage for the man, and his wistful look jolted me into the realisation that he wanted a second chance, another go – just not with me. On the long drive back to Perth we didn't talk much. I think we were both wondering what would happen next.

I found a psychotherapist. The work was intense, painful. Dave eventually agreed to come too, but two sessions were enough for him and he withdrew, saying the issues were mine, not his. At the beginning of 1996, our lives exploded. Our marriage disintegrated, slowly at first and then with alarming speed, as all the unresolved hurts and angers erupted and demanded resolution. I felt strangled, muffled, like I was going to die, like I had to escape. And I did. So did Dave. It was sad, and messy, and very painful. And it occurred at a time in Perth when many people were feeling unsettled, afraid and confused, because of the mysterious disappearances of three young women.

17

Over the roughly eighteen-month period from January 1996 to June 1997, young Perth women Sarah Spiers, Jane Rimmer and Ciara Glennon each went missing, on separate nights, from a popular nightlife strip in the affluent western suburb of Claremont. The bodies of Jane and Ciara were subsequently discovered months after they'd disappeared, but Sarah's remains have never been found.

Sarah was an eighteen-year-old legal secretary who had been out with her mates celebrating Australia Day on the evening of 26 January 1996, when she vanished. Jane, a twenty-three-year-old childcare worker, went missing six months later, after drinks with friends at a nightspot near where Sarah was last seen. Six weeks later her body was found in bushland in Wellard, some forty kilometres south of the Perth CBD. Eight months after Jane's body was discovered, twenty-seven-year-old lawyer Ciara also went missing after celebratory drinks at a Claremont pub. She had just returned home after a year overseas, was settling into a new job and preparing to be a bridesmaid at her sister's wedding. Three weeks later, her body was found in bushland at Eglinton, around forty kilometres north of the Perth CBD.

The suspected serial killings sparked Australia's longest-running police investigation. My own daughters were at that time just spreading their wings and I, along with thousands of other Perth parents, held my breath every time they ventured out at night, breathing again only when they returned safely.

In 1996, immediately after Jane Rimmer's disappearance, Western Australia police established the Macro Task Force to investigate what at that stage were two disappearances but would soon become three – two of which were subsequently confirmed as murders. Because investigators thought there may be a link, with all three women having told friends they were seeking late-night transport home, suspicion initially focused on Perth's taxidrivers. This line of enquiry saw more than two thousand drivers DNA- and character/background-tested, with no apparent results. Police then focused for several years on a particular suspect who had attracted their attention during a decoy operation. Although he appeared to have solid alibis, they spent significant resources on his surveillance until, in 2008, they declared him no longer a person of interest. The mayor of Claremont at the time of the murders then came under investigation, because of his links to a taxidriver who claimed to have given Sarah Spiers a lift, but nothing came of this line of enquiry either. There were other leads in this time, but all came to nothing.

I remember little of the news headlines about the case over these years, because by the end of 1996 I was no longer living in Perth, my girls were overseas and it all seemed far away and not very relevant to me.

18

When my marriage to Dave broke apart in early 1996, each member of our family seemed to go their separate ways. Over the ensuing few years, Dave established a new relationship with a police colleague, and they married in 1998. Two of our daughters, Kate and Jo, travelled to the UK to explore the world outside Australia, and the third, Martha, moved out to live with friends while she finished her university studies. They were all leaving home, and so was I.

Late in 1996, I moved to the Goldfields town of Kalgoorlie to join Tim, an old university friend and colleague. We were both working for the Disability Services Commission, spending time together at meetings, and our relationship had begun to develop into something deeper than friendship. Building on the values and interests we'd shared as friends, we were beginning to see a future together.

It was an intensely exciting time for me. I felt young and strong again, able to do anything, after all the emotional upheaval of my marriage breakdown. I still remember the feeling of absolute euphoria as I drove, trailer in tow, Flossie the old Rottweiler by my side and cats on the back seat, further and further inland through miles and miles of beautiful country, to establish a new life.

That time in Kalgoorlie was healing for me. The relative quiet away from the busy city was so refreshing. Tim and I regularly drove back and forth from Kalgoorlie to the southern coastal town of Esperance, through kilometres of changing landscapes that took our breath away as we rounded a corner or crested a hill. On holidays, we drove to the west coast and swam and fished in the crystal-clear ocean. We walked all around the adjacent towns of Kalgoorlie and Boulder. We walked everywhere. We marvelled at the old houses, the historic deserted mining settlements, the beautiful old architecture – and the roses. Someone once told me that Kalgoorlie has the perfect climate for roses, and they were magnificent. In full bloom, you could smell their different scents as you walked by the massive fragrant blossoms tumbling over fences.

Sometime after Tim and I moved there, one of Tim's sisters also moved to Kalgoorlie for work, and I started to get to know his family. Jo, my youngest daughter, came and stayed for a while too, working three jobs to save money to travel to the UK along with her eldest sister Kate.

By late 1997, both Kate and Jo were in the UK, working. I was happy that they were exploring the world, but they had been away for a while and I was missing them terribly. Technology in those days was not like it is now: there was no Facebook and no Skype. A week or so before Christmas that year, they teamed up for a telephone chat and promised to call me again on Christmas Day. My middle daughter, Martha, was planning to spend Christmas with friends in Perth. Tim and I, however, would not be alone, as Tim's family would all be joining his sister in Kalgoorlie, nieces and nephews included.

It was Christmas Eve, unbearably hot, and Tim and I had just settled outside for a pre-dinner drink. The breeze was blowing cool through the overhead sprinkler system, and we could hear the crows squawking noisily as they settled down for the night. Work had been busy for both of us in the lead-up to Christmas, and we'd planned a quiet night in preparation for the coming day's festivities. Flossie was snoozing by the back door when suddenly, she raised her head and listened. There was a knock at the front door. Tim and I looked at each other. We weren't expecting anyone. I walked inside, dog at my heels. Maybe it was some friends who'd been passing, or the neighbours dropping in for a Christmas Eve drink. The dog was now trotting ahead of me, wagging her tail furiously, having obviously recognised whoever was outside. As I opened the door and peered through the security screen, three voices called out, 'Merry Christmas!' The back door slammed as, recognising the voices, Tim rushed inside. I was speechless, bolted to the floor, tears welling in my eyes. My daughters were all there, on the other side of the locked flywire door. All I could do was stare at them in disbelief. They were smiling, crying, and shouting: 'Merry Christmas! Open the door, Mum! Let us in!' It was the best present I have ever had.

That Christmas was full of hugging and loving and tears, and the beginning of lots of new relationships within our combining families. It would be the last Christmas with everyone from both families together that we would have for eighteen years.

So, life was good. My daughters were spreading their wings. Kate finished her undergraduate studies in psychology and started working with people with disabilities; Martha moved overseas to work, spending years in the UK and eventually coming back to settle in Hobart with a Scottish husband; and Jo moved east for a while. It was during this time that I reverted to my birth surname of Davis, the final step in reclaiming my independence, my sense of self. I now find it so hard to believe that I gave my name away – not once, but twice!

The only niggling negative was Tim's health. He had begun experiencing vague and weird symptoms that would come and go. We convinced ourselves that it was nothing serious, and saw only what we wanted to see.

19

The weeks after Katy and Brendan's visit to Tasmania in February 2017 passed relatively peacefully. Tim and I both sometimes searched online for 'Claremont serial killer – latest news', to make sure we hadn't missed anything. We were aware that Edwards had made three court appearances since his arrest in late 2016, each of which had resulted in an adjournment due to the complexity of the case. And always at the back of my mind was a heavy, sad feeling for the families of his victims.

Katy and Brendan's visit did, however, spark much almost subconscious reflection in me over the next few months. Many seemingly minor but strangely unsettling events that had happened over the years began to make more sense to me now. Once, years ago, Dave and I had been at a quiet restaurant in North Perth, waiting for friends to join us for a meal before we went to the cinema. We were seated close to the kitchen door at the back of the restaurant, and because it was early, we were the only patrons. I was drinking a beer and watching Dave, who had left the table to go to the toilet. I heard a noise coming from the kitchen behind me and a sudden feeling of agitation, almost panic, swept over me: I had my back to the kitchen door. Quickly, I swept up my belongings and swapped places with Dave so that I had visual access to the whole of the room. When Dave returned, he joked about the seat swap. I told him I needed to see all the doors, but I couldn't explain why. He said it was his job to keep an eye on things – he was the policeman, not me.

Another incident was one that had disturbed me not long after Tim and I had moved to Tasmania, but was now more understandable in the light of Edwards' arrest and my subsequent recollection of his face. Tim and I had been caring for my daughter's dog while she was studying overseas. Every day, I walked the dog to the nearby dog beach and chatted to other dog owners while he chased his ball. I became familiar with all the 'regulars', I knew all the dogs, and the outing was a regular, relaxing and enjoyable part of my day. One cool, windy day, the beach was almost empty when I arrived. The water appeared grey, wavelets lapping at the sand, and petrels cawed as they circled and landed in the shallow water for a rest after their long flight across the Southern Ocean. For some reason I felt a sense of unease and slight anxiety at the lack of people around. I became aware of a young man standing at the edge of the park adjoining the beach. He didn't have a dog and, although he did nothing out of the ordinary, I was convinced that he meant me harm. I hurried home, glancing behind me now and then to check that I wasn't being followed. Later, when I spoke about the incident to Tim, I was unable to articulate why I'd felt so uneasy about this person. Tim thought I was imagining things, and I tried to let it go, but my anxiety persisted for the rest of the day and led to a sleepless night. The reason for my unease was now obvious. That young man had been tall and, with waves of dark hair framing his face, resembled Bradley Edwards – the man I had eradicated so successfully from my conscious memory.

There had been other times.

The tall, dark-haired man with a white cloth in his hand, leaning against a white van parked in our street. I approached to walk past him, a bag of shopping in each hand. The pavement and the street were narrow, echoes of old Hobart Town a hundred years ago. As I got closer, he turned and opened the van door. I froze, my heart pounding in my chest, unable to decide whether to continue past him or run across the road. He blew his nose loudly. It was okay. It was just a handkerchief.

Sitting in the garden at Tim's mum's house on our first trip to Tassie. Drinking coffee and getting to know my mother-in-law. Misty rain. It was very cold. We had our beanies on. I could feel that we were making a connection. She went inside for a moment and I savoured the quiet, smelt the rain. Miles away, I didn't hear her come back out. Instead, I felt her hands gently on my shoulders. She was behind me, saying something, but I was paralysed. I knew it was her, but for a moment I couldn't breathe. She spoke again: 'Are you okay? Sorry – did I startle you?'

I might have tried to bury what had happened all those years ago, but I was starting to understand the impact it had had on my life anyway. And now, a quarter of a century after the event, I could feel the suppressed trauma thrusting its way to the surface, unstoppable.

* * *

Towards the end of the summer of early 2017, I planned a trip to Perth to visit my daughter Kate and my now seven-month-old granddaughter, a much-wanted baby who'd been born the previous year to Kate and her husband, Damon, who had married in 2009. I also informed Katy that I was coming, and she suggested we catch up while I was in town. I agreed. I like to think they were keeping a bit of any eye on me, making sure I was travelling okay. I also thought they would update me on the proceedings as far as they were able.

When they came for coffee at my daughter's house, the detectives' update was brief, with little new information. They were hard at work processing reams of evidence, they told me, and it would be many months before Edwards would face trial. They were unable to confirm at this stage whether I would be called as a witness, whether my potential appearance might be required in person or by video link, or how Edwards was likely to plead.

I was interested in how Edwards was responding to his current incarceration and the impending proceedings. They told me his stepdaughter visited him in prison, that the story was extremely hard for her to believe, but they were unable, of course, to give me any more detailed information. I wondered about his parents, his mother. Was she disbelieving? Supportive of her son? Or was she devastated, grieving, wondering what part she might have played in this terrible drama?

They had made some enlarged copies of the photographs I had given them, and I studied them once again. Those pretty maroon-coloured shoes were a reminder, a symbol of a terrifying event that had changed my life not once, but twice now.

20

Towards the end of 1998, Tim and I bought a dual-cab ute, packed all our belongings, said goodbye to our families, friends and workmates in Kalgoorlie and set off on a long trek around the country. We were so happy. Tim's mother and stepfather had just retired to Tasmania after many years in the mining industry on the mainland, and Tim was keen to spend some time with his mum for the first time in many years. Sadly, as with my own mother, within a few short years breast cancer was to take her life.

On our journey we visited my brother and some old friends of Tim's. They were all meeting us as a couple for the first time, so there was lots of celebrating, new people to meet and new places to explore. It was not, however, all smooth sailing. Relaxing in a cabin after a day's exploring in the Warrumbungle Range in New South Wales, we received a telephone call with devastating news. It was Jo. Her voice was trembling. Her father – Dave – had been diagnosed with oesophageal cancer and was terribly ill. They were all in shock and couldn't seem to process the news. Having worked in palliative care, I was very aware that this was a dangerous cancer, fast spreading and with only a small chance of survival. Unsure of what to do, we continued with our trip and arrived in Tasmania a week or so later. Within a short time of arriving, we had both obtained work, but daily phone contact with my daughters indicated that things were not going well with Dave and they needed support – they needed their mum. And so, after only two months in our new home, we packed up and headed back to Western Australia.

Crossing the Nullarbor again, this time westwards, we received a phone call from a colleague in the Disability Services Commission. The news was out that we were returning to Perth, and we were told that there were jobs waiting for us both. We were so very grateful.

* * *

The next six months were filled with sadness. Despite undergoing gruelling chemotherapy, Dave grew steadily weaker and sicker. Just a week before he died, Tim's mysterious symptoms were finally given a label: he had multiple sclerosis.

It was a time of terrible grief. There were many family gatherings at our house, lots of tears, hugs, and late-night conversations fuelled with Tim's curries, beer and wine. We all sensed that this was a time of change, and we were all working out how to manage ourselves and perhaps wondering just what our family would look like in the next few years. Where would we all be? I didn't know it at the time, but that was to be one of the last times I was together with my girls for the next seven years.

* * *

Six months after Dave died, Tim and I married, in 2000. With my daughters all still in Perth, we thought it would be a positive thing to have something healing and joyful to celebrate after all the heartache. We had never turned our backs on Tasmania, though. For both of us, our short time there had felt like coming home. After a brief period in Bridgetown in the south-west of Western Australia, in 2004 we packed up again and headed back eastwards over the Nullarbor, determined this time to make the Apple Isle our home.

Towards justice

1

I remember when my sister-in-law, Jan, called us in Hobart in early 2018 to let us know that Bradley Edwards had now also been charged with the murder of Sarah Spiers. She referred to him as 'that monster' and, as she spoke, several questions whirled around in my head. Would the Spiers family now finally be able to lay their daughter to rest? Would Edwards plead guilty? Would there be a trial? The previous six months had seen a gradual subsidence of the trauma that had re-emerged for me following Edwards' initial arrest, but this news of the new charge brought it back with a vengeance. I felt nauseous, slightly apprehensive, drawn back into the ever-evolving story that was once again dominating the Perth media.

It was in February 2018, fourteen months after he was first arrested, that Edwards appeared in court by video link to hear the new charge. The public gallery was packed with people, including the families of his alleged victims. Because of the new charge and the need to examine more than a million pages of evidence, the case was adjourned until late July.

I was now sixty-eight years old, and it seemed to me that time was moving at an ever-increasing pace. I could almost feel it passing, like being on a river that speeds up as it approaches a waterfall. For me, the dichotomy that this adjournment represented was palpable: five months 'break' to go back to normal life, but at the same time five months with the heavy looming cloud of unfinished business circling overhead, slightly muffling my thoughts, affecting my actions, like a continuous noise running in the background. My heart ached for the other living victims, and for the family members of those slain. The path towards justice can be slow and brutal.

There was little further news after the new charge, and I sometimes wondered what life was like at this time for Bradley Edwards, safe in Hakea Prison on Perth's outskirts, where he had been held on remand since his arrest, presumably participating in the dreary routine of prison life. Did he think about the things he had allegedly done, things that were so awful they were unimaginable for most of us? Was he measuring his life by the atrocities committed? Was he reliving them, piece by piece, trying to gain some understanding of himself? Did he have any idea of the impact those actions had had on so many people, the cost to the community in every way? Was he contemplating his personal relationships, his career, his community involvement, acutely aware that they had all changed now? Now that he had been called out for being an imposter. Now that technology had caught up with him. Now that people were piecing together his escalatingly violent criminal career. Or, unthinkably, had the police got it wrong? Was it remotely possible that he was innocent?

At the end of June that year, I organised another visit to Perth for the following month, to see my eldest daughter, spend some time with my granddaughter and catch up with my friends. A few days after I'd made my arrangements, a text message arrived from Katy, offering to provide an update. She said she was unsure whether we were following the events or trying to block them out. I called and told her we couldn't help but be interested, that the closer it got to trial, the more intense my involvement felt. She said I could expect a letter from the Office of the Director of Public Prosecutions (DPP) soon, detailing the proceedings and expectations. They would want to see me regarding my witness statement, she said, to ensure all was as it should be. We agreed to catch up for a coffee while I was in Perth and, as the call finished, I suddenly realised that I would be there when Edwards went back to court.

As the weeks and months continued to pass, I could feel myself being drawn further into the sinister world of the serial killer. Because it had now touched me in a very personal way, I was, for the first time, beginning to understand some people's fascination with the terrible, the horrific. I began tuning in to true crime shows on Foxtel, Netflix and YouTube, binge-watching TV while Maisie moped around looking reproachful, trying to persuade me to take her out for a walk.

In an effort to understand both what had happened all those years ago and what was happening now as the case progressed, I searched the internet for information about the Claremont killings. However, apart from resurrecting the originally published details about the murders, the Western Australian media were strangely silent. Were they, I wondered, being respectful of the judicial process or under instructions to avoid printing anything that could jeopardise what was shaping up in Perth to be the trial of the century? I found little to study, nothing to bring me closer to understanding either the modus operandi or the motivation associated with the crimes allegedly committed by Bradley Edwards.

I could find little information about his family, either. It seemed that he and his brother had grown up in the Gosnells area, not far from where we'd lived in Kelmscott. I wondered what sort of relationship they had. What were their parents like? Were they a happy family? Did they have any suspicions about their eldest son and brother? Did he have lots of friends, or was he a loner? And how on earth were they all managing to deal with his arrest? How do you accept that your son, your brother, your friend is an alleged serial killer? Perhaps it was just all too hard to contemplate and they were supporting him in the hope that a long and detailed trial would prove him innocent, vindicate him of all wrongdoing.

* * *

In my ongoing search for knowledge and context, I discovered a book about the Claremont killings that had been published in 2007, a decade after the discovery of the bodies of Jane Rimmer and Ciara Glennon but well before an arrest had been made. *The Devil's Garden* was written by Debi Marshall, a journalist and author whose own partner was brutally murdered in 1992. Detailing all the knowledge she could glean from many sources about the killings, Debi wrote about their impacts on the families of the victims, and the ongoing investigations conducted by the Western Australia Police Force, of which she was at times scathing. She also detailed several miscarriages of justice in the WA legal system that were exposed in the years following the Claremont killings. In her preface, she wrote that her research sought to discover whether 'these dreadful killings are still unsolved due to police incompetence, the sheer brilliance of the killer to escape detection, or just plain bad luck'. My own experience with Edwards suggested there might be an element of all three.

Debi also wrote, in the introduction to her book, that she 'felt patronised by a pervading male culture, the boys club', when dealing with the WA police force. These words resonated particularly strongly with me. I vividly remember receiving a very clear message about the expectations associated with my future life as a policeman's wife – a message that I didn't really take heed of at the time, but one that would come back to me in later years as I sometimes struggled to be a 'good' wife. The message was delivered at Dave's graduation from the Western Australia Police Academy in July 1978. He was dux of his year, it was a special occasion and, heavily pregnant with our second child, I was enormously proud of him. During the celebratory festivities after the ceremony I was in the change rooms with my fifteen-month-old toddler, washing my hands, when an older woman in police uniform started chatting to me about the stresses of police life, how important their job was, how difficult 'the boys' found it sometimes, and that the most important thing was for them to always have their wife and family in full support. Nodding and placing my hand over my swollen belly as I felt my baby moving inside me, I took my little one's hand to lead her back outside and the woman followed me, still talking. She went on to say that it might be very hard for me sometimes, that Dave would often be away or stressed, but that I should always make allowances for him and that I would be making a great contribution to his work if I was able to put my own needs aside, look after him and be a strong police wife.

I was married to Dave for twenty years, and during that time I always felt totally shut out of his work environment. The strong emphasis on mateship, teamwork, all the associated police-only socialisation and Friday-night drinks with 'the boys' significantly affected our family life, particularly when the children were younger. Add in shift work, overtime and, in Dave's case, intensive postgraduate study and I often felt very much like a single parent, a sort of machine-mother juggling all the responsibilities necessary to keep the family functioning, trying desperately to retain some sense of myself as a person, doing everything for everyone else with as little fuss as possible.

I found Debi's book both enlightening and depressing. As part of her investigations she'd interviewed Robin Napper, a former UK detective and head of operations for the UK's National Crime Agency who had worked on several cold-case murder reviews in the UK in the mid-1990s. In 1998, then New South Wales police commissioner Peter Ryan had invited Napper to Australia to share his forensic investigative skills – in particular his valued knowledge of then-emerging DNA technology – with his Australian counterparts. Then in 2001 Napper had been appointed director of Marketing and Development at the University of Western Australia's Centre for Forensic Science, where he'd helped to develop a forensic science program for students. Working on several cases that had been dealt with by the WA legal system, he'd highlighted poor investigation techniques that had resulted in significant miscarriages of justice.

Napper explained to Debi that serial killers generally build up to their 'peak performance', that they are familiar with their killing environment, and that their work or social life often takes them to their killing and dumping grounds. He maintained that the Claremont killer would have detailed knowledge of both Claremont and the outlying areas where the bodies of Jane and Ciara had been discarded, and that police should be focusing on the links between these areas. He also suggested a thorough search of previous assaults and unusual criminal behaviour during the years preceding the killings. In 2004 Napper recommended a cold-case review of the Claremont killings involving criminal and geographic profilers, pathologists, forensic experts and forensic archaeologists, even suggesting the experts whom he considered to be the best in each of these fields. According to Debi, however, Western Australia police closed ranks against Napper, ignoring his advice and continuing with their own outdated methods of investigation.

My heart sank when I read this. Had WA police listened to Napper, I thought, they might have made some connections earlier, if only someone had understood that both the kimono incident in Huntingdale and the attack on me were unusual forms of violence – the type of behaviour that might pre-empt an escalation to eventual killing.

Napper was not the only person Debi interviewed who questioned the investigation. Western Australian barrister John Quigley – who in 2017 would become the state's attorney-general – told her that some police investigators not associated with the Macro Task Force felt that the investigation was too narrow. It was chilling for me to read that one such investigator had observed to Quigley that the Macro Task Force should have urgently requested from all local police stations in the area a copy of every record relating to 'any act of perversion' in Claremont and surrounding suburbs during the period in question.

When he'd attacked me, Edwards had been charged with common assault. When the task force had begun its investigations into the murders, it had looked at other crimes in the area, but only at 'serious' crimes such as rape and sexual assault. It had never expanded these investigations to cover all assaults, or to look further back, despite Napper's advice and the vast amounts of money that were poured into the case over the first decade after the murders.

Thinking about the revelations made in Debi's book, I could feel another resurgence of the frustration and hurt that I'd experienced all those years ago when I'd felt unheard. Ignoring Robin Napper's advice – that serial killers practise before they kill, that they commit other violent crimes in the lead-up to their ultimate crimes, that investigators should expand their search, should look further back, should look at other crimes in nearby areas – the police had been unaware that the killer was already on record.

2

When the letter from the Office of the DPP arrived, it was hand-delivered by our postman. He pulled up on his motorcycle outside our gate just as Maisie and I arrived home from a long, relaxed, happy walk in the sunshine. I took the letter and, as I walked inside, made coffee and settled myself down to read it, I realised that my light mood of that morning had been replaced with a seriousness, and a tension hovered in the air around me.

Titled *The State of Western Australia v Bradley Robert Edwards*, the letter was from Carmel Barbagallo SC, Deputy Director of the DPP. She stated that she was responsible for the overall management and conduct of the prosecution, and headed a small team of prosecutors and paralegals from the directorate. She formally acknowledged the trauma caused to me by the 'violent and frightening conduct of Bradley Edwards on May 7, 1990, at Hollywood Hospital', and thanked me for my current cooperation.

As I read her words, my mind returned to the police report that had been presented to the court after Edwards' attack on me, but which I had only seen for the first time when Katy and Brendan had visited me in Hobart in 2017. That report had resulted in a very minor conviction that had hardly affected Edwards' life, and that certainly did not appear to have acted as a deterrent to him in any way. For me, however, it had triggered a chain of events that had affected my career and my personal relationships and left me with a lack of respect and trust for the police force and for our legal system in general. Katy and

Brendan were the first people to have really listened and understood what had happened to me. Carmel Barbagallo's acknowledgement had now provided me with some formal reassurance that, nearly three decades later, things had changed, and my experience was finally being validated.

The letter went on to detail the current state of affairs, advising that the next court date would be 25 July 2018, when a request would be made in the Stirling Gardens Magistrates Court to commit all charges to the Supreme Court and have provisional trial dates set aside should the matter proceed to trial. If it did, it was anticipated that the trial would be a lengthy one.

The first hearing in the Supreme Court was expected to be sometime in September or October, and other hearing dates would follow. I would not be required to attend any of these unless I received a witness summons from the DPP, served by Tasmania Police. If I did, I might be required to provide evidence for one or more days and on one or more occasions. Beforehand there would be a pre-trial conference which, in my case, would likely occur by videoconference. This would be an opportunity to discuss my evidence and clarify any questions or concerns I might have.

It seemed there was a potential alternative to providing evidence in the courtroom. The letter stated that the prosecution could apply to the Supreme Court for me to be declared a 'special witness' if it could be shown that I was unable to give evidence in the courtroom, either because it would cause me 'severe emotional trauma' or because I would be too 'intimidated or distressed' to properly provide evidence. In such a case, the letter explained, I may be permitted to give my evidence from a 'remote room' separate from the courtroom. This might not be in Tasmania but could be in Perth. Everyone in the courtroom would still be able to view me on a television screen, but I would only be able to see the judge and the prosecution and defence lawyers. Such an application would require professional medical or psychological support, and would need to be considered by the relevant Supreme Court Justice.

Should I request this, I wondered? Which option would be best for me? Which would be best for the case? I would consider my decision over the coming months.

There was also an attachment to the letter, from the prosecution team, requesting witness contact details and availability for the whole of 2019. Tim and I had no major travel plans that would take us away from home, but we were not used to planning that far ahead – we tended to just take a week's break when we felt we needed a change of scenery.

Finally, it felt as though things were moving. I wondered who else might be receiving similar letters, who else might possibly be called as witnesses. Edwards' other living victims? His wives? His friends and colleagues? Would there be lots of forensic experts? Would there be others who now lived interstate? People from overseas? I had so many questions. There was so much I didn't know.

With the letter from the DPP moving everything up a notch, I was beginning to feel overwhelmed by the enormity of the impending trial. I wondered how I would cope with organising any necessary time away, possibly at short notice. Where would I stay? Would Tim be okay at home alone, now that things were becoming more difficult for him physically? Or would he perhaps be able to manage the journey, now that the airlines were introducing direct flights from Hobart to Perth? If we both went, what would we do with Maisie? And, most importantly, would I cope emotionally? Or would it all be too much, after all these years, to relive that long-ago but still terrifying attack in front of the person who had actually done it? The person who would now be on trial for killing three women and brutally raping another.

3

I flew to Western Australia in mid-July 2018, and enjoyed a week of much-anticipated time with my eldest daughter and granddaughter. They lived in a sheltered, secluded part of Perth, close to the river and to parklands, a little bubble that seemed completely isolated from what has become the fast, busy, and very modern face of Perth. Children played in the quiet, leafy cul-de-sac, cats jumped the dividing walls to visit their neighbours, and occasionally a car drove slowly past, looking for parking or just admiring the tall townhouses. Only the faint hum of traffic provided a clue that we were just five minutes from the CBD.

I didn't hear from Katy or the DPP for the first few days of my visit, so I assumed they didn't want to meet with me at that stage. Immersed in family life, in holiday mode and out of touch with time, I even forgot the date of Edwards' court appearance. Visiting my friend Sheila, I was jolted back to reality when I caught the news on television. The sound was off as I watched the families of the women whom Edwards was alleged to have murdered leaving the Magistrates Court. They looked stoic, grim. I could not even begin to imagine what they must be going through, how everything must be flooding back after all these years, like a horror movie being replayed over and over. I turned the sound on. Edwards had just pleaded not guilty to three charges of murder, one of rape and one of assault. I felt sick, angry and disbelieving all at once. As I watched and listened, I was overcome by the same feelings of frustration, despair and powerlessness I'd felt in the aftermath of the attack all those years ago. Why was he putting all these people through this? Surely he must be aware that there was enough evidence to convict him? Surely there wasn't a chance that he was innocent? I could only hope that this time the system would punish him properly, that he wouldn't escape with a lesser conviction, that his victims and their families would finally get justice.

Having thus been shaken out of the reverie of my holiday, I felt it might be good to meet with Katy to get an update and a sense of perspective. I texted her, and immediately everything swung into action. Within twenty-four hours she had arranged a meeting with the DPP for the day before I was due to fly back home to Hobart. It was on again.

When Katy picked me up she asked me how I was going, and I said I was okay. But the reality was that I'd found it difficult to get to sleep the previous night. My mind had been going round and round, the events of twenty-eight years ago becoming enmeshed with everything that had happened over the past two years. I was anxious inside, slightly manic on the outside. I wondered what the prosecutors would ask me today, what questions I should ask. I worried that I would become emotional. This was very new ground for me.

Katy was businesslike, reassuring. This was all familiar territory for her, and she knew all the people we were about to see. She told me that we would be meeting with Brad Hollingsworth, the Assistant Deputy Chief Prosecutor, since Carmel Barbagallo, the Deputy Chief Prosecutor who was managing the case, was on holiday, trekking in Iceland. I thought perhaps Ms Barbagallo needed to be so far away, in such a different environment, to leave it all behind for just a bit and, for a moment, I really envied her.

We arrived at the DPP building overlooking the Swan River, went through security, and stepped into the domain of the law. There was a feeling of high energy, a sense of purpose. All the men were in suits, all the women wearing high heels, and I felt very out of place. Smiling at a friendly-looking man, Katy introduced me to Joe, who ushered us into the lift and up to the top floor. I had read that one whole floor of this building was being used to manage the massive amount of evidence that was to be presented at Edwards' trial. Katy and Joe chatted on the way up in the lift, trying to include me in the conversation, but I was preoccupied with my preparation for what felt like an interview – for what, I was unsure, but I felt that I needed to do well, that the outcome of this meeting was important.

When the lift opened there was light everywhere, and big glass doors led us through to a long office with such a magnificent view of the Swan River that it took my breath away. I commented how incredible it must be to work in such a beautiful environment. But then as I adjusted to the room, I became aware of it as a working office. Documents were piled high on desks, on the floor. There was a sense of bustle, of business. I imagined that those who worked there appreciated the calming panoramic outlook, and maybe it helped them to cope with their workloads and maintain some perspective. It couldn't be easy, dealing all the time with people who have stretched the accepted limits of human behaviour, hearing the stories of victims of sometimes very violent crimes, and endeavouring to administer justice.

Katy introduced me to Brad Hollingsworth and the rest of the prosecution team, who were expecting me. Someone offered me tea, and we all went into a meeting room. I was glad Katy was there. Brad began by explaining that he would give me an update on the proceedings so far, and outline how future proceedings might affect me. He would share all the information he was able to, he said. I understood, of course, that there were many details that he would not be at liberty to impart. I resolved to try to remember everything he told me, but my mind was already leaping ahead, wondering just what would be expected of me. Brad emphasised that I was welcome to interrupt him at any time, and that he would attempt to answer any questions I might have. I relaxed a little as he reiterated the sympathy expressed in the original letter from Carmel Barbagallo, and acknowledged that I had indeed been the victim of a violent crime.

Holding tightly to this validation, I listened as Brad summarised the events since Edwards' arrest. Most of the information he shared was already in the public domain or had been set out in the letter from the DPP, but I found it particularly useful to hear it all ordered chronologically.

Brad stressed that the DPP team was making every effort to maintain my privacy and keep my name out of the public domain. However, because this was such a high-profile case, they were understandably concerned that the media would find my story very interesting. Because of this, to ensure that there was no interference in the trial process and to protect my privacy and that of Edwards' other living victims and other prosecution witnesses, they would apply for suppression orders at Edwards' next court appearance, which was scheduled for mid-September. This would effectively block the media from publishing my name or any personal details about me. I was relieved to hear this. At this stage I had not considered telling my story publicly, and I certainly did not want to influence the trial process in any way.

Brad went on to explain that the prosecution team intended to request a judge-only trial. Their reasoning was that it was unlikely that Edwards would be able to face an unbiased jury, given that it was such a high-profile case and had been such a long-running investigation. Another factor was the complicated nature of the mountains of forensic evidence that needed to be analysed and assessed. With professional knowledge of court proceedings and of the evaluation of scientific evidence, an experienced judge was more likely to correctly interpret the evidence than a cross-section of inexperienced community members.

As Brad spoke, I listened carefully, nodding and commenting now and again to confirm that I acknowledged and understood what he was saying. I asked questions to clarify the details of my potential involvement, and told him I was prepared to assist in any way I could to help with the case against Edwards. I think everyone in that room could see that I wanted to be heard.

The prosecution's application to present my evidence would not be made until November, Brad explained, and there was the possibility that the defence would oppose it. The prosecution team, however, felt that it was relevant because, along with the evidence from the other two assaults, it would show a pattern of escalating violence typical of serial killers. I was asked whether I was planning to take any holidays or have any surgery in the coming year. Smiling faintly, I said no to the former and hopefully not to the latter.

Reiterating the information in the letter from Carmel Barbagallo, Brad told me that, if I was required to present evidence, I could apply to be declared a special witness and permitted to give my evidence by video link, if a medical professional could confirm that facing Edwards in court might cause me severe psychological distress. However, given the seriousness of the case and the public interest, even if permission for this was granted the judge might very well order that it be done in Perth rather than in Hobart. Brad also explained that I might be required to attend court more than once, and at short notice, so these were all things I would need to keep in mind over the following months.

As far as I was concerned, I was starting to feel that this would all be manageable. It would all be far less difficult for me than the process the families of Sarah, Jane and Ciara must already be navigating. As for the other two women, who had been so young when they were assaulted, I wondered how they were coping.

My cup sat on the table, still half-full of now stone-cold tea. I was flagging. It had been an intense hour, and I could sense that the meeting was coming to an end. Brad asked me whether I would be bringing a support person with me if and when I was called to give evidence. I said yes, my husband would probably come. He said that our travel expenses would be taken care of, but since this trial had already cost the taxpayer so much money, maybe we could stay with my daughter? I looked at him but did not answer. I was too tired to explain that Tim has MS, that he therefore has mobility issues and was unable to negotiate the three flights of stairs in my daughter's house.

Before we finished, Brad emphasised again that the media would have an intense interest in the trial and, should I be contacted by anyone, I should let the prosecution team know so they could advise me.

I asked one more question. When would the trial start? Brad said they were doing everything in their power to have it finished by Christmas the following year, which meant a start date of 1 May 2019. This terrible drama had dragged on for so many years they all felt, for the sake of the families and everyone else involved, it would be good to have some form of closure by the end of 2019. I very much hoped that would be the case.

As Katy and I made our way back to her car through the bustling Perth streets, I glanced at passers-by going about their business and wished I was having an ordinary day too. But I wasn't. I felt burdened and a little battered by what had been and by what was to come.

4

After Edwards' July 2018 appearance in the Perth Magistrates Court, where he'd entered pleas of not guilty to all charges, I received another letter from Carmel Barbagallo. It was much briefer than the first and it informed me that Edwards had now been committed to the Supreme Court to appear on 17 September, and that now that the matter was in the Supreme Court, they anticipated 'numerous appearances and hearing dates for the determination of legal argument and other administrative matters'. Anticipating a trial commencement in May 2019, Ms Barbagallo reiterated the basic information provided in the first letter, stressing that I needed to inform them of any changes in my availability to attend court.

September 2018 brought unseasonably warm and dry weather to Hobart. In our garden, the trees and plants were starting to wake up from their winter hibernation, the blackbirds were out looking for worms in the moist soil, and I could see the first leaves on the neighbours' apple trees. I smiled as I watched Tim watering the backyard, our two-year-old granddaughter tagging behind him, chattering away and 'helping' with her little watering can. Maisie trailed close behind them both, interested in everything the little one was doing, and I felt content, happy with my lot in life.

I was aware that Edwards' first appearance in the Supreme Court by video link from Hakea prison was scheduled for that day. Busy organising lunch, my thoughts drifted once again to the families of

Sarah, Jane and Ciara. Would they be there to see the man who had stolen the lives of their beautiful young women, or was it all just too much for them to bear? It was now nearly two years since Edwards had been arrested. I was certain that the proceedings since then would have been agonising for them, reigniting their original feelings of grief, horror and despair. Were they also feeling some sense of relief as things moved forward, or perhaps frustration because the pace was so slow? And what about the other two young women who had been assaulted by Edwards prior to his killing spree – were they in court that day? Were they there studying the face of the man who had so viciously attacked them? Or were they, like me, watching from a distance, trying to come to terms with their fortunate escape?

I'd put my granddaughter down for a nap and was taking a break, enjoying a coffee in a sunny sheltered spot in the yard, when my phone chimed and Brad Hollingsworth's name came up. His voice was tight, controlled, and he sounded stressed. He asked if this was a good time to talk, as he would like to update me on the court appearance. He talked for fifteen minutes, and I tried to take it all in, but it was hard because he was obviously very busy and each piece of information he gave set off a chain of reactions in my mind.

He told me that the court was packed to overflowing in both the public and press galleries, that it was a total 'media circus', that I was lucky to be so far away. Judge Michael Corby would be managing the case leading up to the trial, and both Sarah Spiers' and Ciara Glennon's fathers were present, as they had been at every appearance since Edwards' arrest.

Edwards was facing a total of eight charges. I wondered whether that meant there were more victims, but I didn't ask, thinking that the news reports would surely cover that. The defence now had the full prosecution details. The prosecutors had told the court that they had filed an application for the trial to be heard by judge alone, without a jury. That application was to be heard on 1 October; the defence team would then have until late October to file submissions relating to the application. I wondered what Edwards' preference would be. Would he simply agree to a judge-only trial, or would he want twelve of his peers whom he could potentially influence and persuade that he was not a bad man, that he really was the upstanding community member he'd appeared to be for the past twenty-five years?

Brad told me that several suppression orders relating to the non-identification of a number of people likely to be involved in the trial, including potential prosecution witnesses, had been granted. The applications, read out in court, included my current surname and my surname at the time of the attack. He went on to say that the order would prevent any publication of my name and of the names that had not yet been released of Edwards' other living victims. Somewhat relieved, I also understood that the order would not necessarily stop any interested parties from researching my current whereabouts and contacting me. Brad asked me to let him know if that happened. My anxiety rose a notch with those words, but I was hopeful that I was far enough away from the proceedings to be safe from prying questioners.

As I listened to Brad, I thought of the witnesses to my assault. I knew that the police had not contacted the nurse who'd been first on the scene that day as I'd scrambled out of my office, in disarray and complete shock, down the corridor towards the nurses' station. She and I were still in occasional contact, and I was sure that she would have let me know if anyone had spoken with her about what had happened at Hollywood Hospital. I was aware from earlier conversations with Katy and Brendan that they had searched for and managed to locate the locum doctor who'd been on duty on the palliative care ward on the day I was attacked. Hugh was apparently now back in his Irish homeland, practising as a GP, but remembered the incident. They had also managed to locate the hospital security officer who'd been on duty that day. Amazingly, it seemed he still worked at the hospital and remembered the attack very clearly, because it was so unusual and because of the police involvement and resulting criminal charge. I also knew they'd searched for records of the incident in the hospital files. They'd found my letter of resignation. Surely, I thought, there must have been other information on my file. I remembered filling out an incident report. Had there been any information in the hospital's occupational health and safety records, information that perhaps had prompted the hospital to install security alarms at the desks of those working in that office?

As Brad talked, my mind leapt from one thought to another. Because my neck had hurt after the attack, I had made sure that I'd seen a local doctor and requested that the bruises be noted in case of further problems or the need for a worker's compensation claim. Katy had said that she would check with Medicare to access my medical records at the time. Had this been done?

I was aware, thanks to Katy and Brendan, that the outcome of Edwards' 1990 court appearance relating to his attack on me had included probation, a psychiatric assessment and some ongoing counselling. I vaguely recalled that Dave might have passed some of this information on to me at the time but, because I'd been so devastated that my attacker had not been charged with anything more serious, I'd switched off, burying anything relating to him deep down alongside his face and his name. But now I wanted to know everything. What had been the outcome of the psychiatric assessment? Had there been any indication that he was a terribly angry person who lacked the restraint necessary to control his violent urges? Had he received ongoing counselling? Who was the counsellor? Had they gained any understanding of his personality, his weaknesses, his problems? Or had he appeared normal, a young man struggling with relationships and his emotions? A young man with a good job, bright prospects, an apparently loving family who, out of the blue, had violently gagged and restrained an unknown woman around the neck from behind and dragged her towards a secluded, virtually soundproof area of the building. Surely some alarm bells must have rung somewhere? Would the psychiatrist and the counsellor be called as witnesses? Would I find answers to any or all of these questions during the court proceedings?

I took a deep breath and forced my attention back to Brad.

Because Edwards had already faced court for his assault on me, Brad was saying, the prosecution team had had to devise a new category under which to present the application for the suppression order relating to my identity: I was now an 'other victim of offences committed or allegedly committed'. As I listened to this information, it came home to me again that, twenty-eight years earlier, I had been very much a victim: the victim of a callous, sadistic man who had in some way managed to convince the police, his employer and presumably his family that his attack on me was merely a one-off lapse. A man who, it now seemed, had gone on to become a rapist and a murderer.

Brad said there would be another court hearing on 26 September, at which Edwards would be required to formally plead to the charges. Pre-trial applications, including the application for presentation of my evidence, would then take up to two months. Provisional trial dates had now been set for the following May, as originally planned. However, Edwards' defence lawyer, senior barrister Paul Yovich, had indicated that he did not think that date was feasible given the massive brief of evidence to be considered: the material ran to in excess of 1.5 million documents. It seemed that the trial could become an electronic trial with a searchable database of documents for the court to access. So many documents to organise. So much evidence required to ensure a conviction. So many things that could get lost, or go wrong.

Brad said he would keep in touch, keep me informed. As I turned my attention to the tousled little figure just emerging from her nap, my mind was racing, my thoughts scattered, as I tried to process all of the information he had just given me.

5

My regular journalling was helping me to process and understand what was happening with the court proceedings. It was also, perhaps more importantly, enabling me to offload some of the thoughts and flashbacks that had become an ever-increasing part of my life since that first phone call from Katy almost two years earlier. The current year had become increasingly busy with the trial preparations, family life had been hectic, and I felt that I needed some space to document what was happening, to process my emotions. So in October, Tim and I booked a week away in a holiday shack in Eggs and Bacon Bay, a little hamlet on Tasmania's southern coast about an hour's drive from Hobart. I planned to write and walk on the beach, nothing more. My mind needed to concentrate, and my body needed to rest.

When we arrived, it was simply perfect: a mixture of holiday and retirement homes nestled around a sheltered bay with a calm, safe beach. Some of the homes were perched on the headland looking out over Randall's Bay, and the views from there were breathtaking. Our shack was basic but comfortable, with expansive views over the inlet and a log fire that warmed the place to roasting. We took enough supplies to last the week, there was wi-fi and a fenced yard for Maisie. We had everything we needed.

By the second day, deep in memories, I found myself close to tears much of the time. Writing about what had happened all those years ago and what was happening now was painful. As I read over what I had written, I was starting to understand the trauma that had happened to me. I wanted to get it out, to be heard, but at the same time I was battling the urge to forget it all, to stop writing, to push it all back down – I just wanted it all to go away. I knew it wouldn't, though, not until it was finished. There was a story emerging from my notes, an important story and I realised that I wanted to tell it.

Eggs and Bacon Bay is surely one of the most peaceful places in the world. There's no hum of traffic, no reversing beepers, no car alarms going off, no supermarket music, no chattering of people. Nothing disturbed our solitude; the only sounds were the birds and the waves. Fully immersed in the past, I had been writing all day and it was time for a break.

The weather was perfect as Maisie and I walked along the little beach, enjoying the sparkling sunshine and a slight cool breeze. Because it was school holidays, I'd been concerned that the beach might be overrun with people. It wasn't. It was deserted. As we ambled along, I took deep breaths of the crisp clean air and focused on the sun gleaming on the still water. Maisie took advantage of my distraction and headed back to the big dead flathead we'd passed a moment or two before. She rolled around on it in utter glee until it was a big squelchy mess. When she'd had enough, she headed back to me, tail erect and a feral look in her eye. She smelled putrid, and I was just thinking about where in the shack would be the best place to bathe her when a van drove by behind us on the little dirt road just off the beach. I could hear it clearly because everything was so quiet. It went to the end of the little bay, then turned, came back, turned again and parked just ahead of us. I was aware of it. Too aware. I glanced over. The windows were tinted: I couldn't see who was inside. I felt uneasy, and I remembered again how this sort of unsettling incident had happened to me so many times since the attack. I kept glancing at the van, and couldn't decide whether to carry on walking to the end of the beach or return to where we'd started from. Which was the safer option? I heard a click as the van door opened. My heart skipped a beat, and then people piled out, one after another. It was a family – two women and four children. They had come to play on the beach. Everything was okay.

* * *

By early November we were back at home in Hobart. The days were getting longer and Christmas seemed to be fast approaching, the retail industry in full assault mode. Some shops were already displaying decorations, and Christmas specials jumped out at me as I shopped for groceries in the local supermarket. Advertisements in the newspaper and on social media pressured me to buy things for people, things they didn't really want, things they definitely didn't need. We were expecting all the family to be together again this year: Kate and Damon and their now-toddler daughter would be joining us from Perth, and the celebrations were to be at our house so there was lots to do, lots to look forward to.

Around this time there was a flurry of news from the West: texts from Tim's sisters, newspaper headlines and articles from Kate. Edwards had appeared in court in person for the first time. I realised I had lost track of time, but on some level, I had been expecting this. I wondered whether the families and the other living victims were in court. I hoped they all had lots of support, as they would surely need it over the coming months: facing Edwards in person could not be easy.

The media revealed that there would be months of pre-trial legal argument over admissible evidence. For the first time, prosecutors had indicated that this might include 'propensity' evidence, which is evidence of a person's propensity to act in a particular way or to have a particular state of mind – in other words, evidence of previous similar behaviour. I assumed this would include my evidence. The matter would return to court in January.

The day after that court appearance, I was out shopping when I received a call from Brad Hollingsworth. Pushing my trolley to a quiet corner of the supermarket, I listened to the latest update. As with his previous call, Brad sounded stressed and terribly busy. He apologised for not calling me the previous day. I didn't tell him I already knew much of the outcome of the court appearance, as I was hoping he would tell me more. Would I be required to give evidence? Would it be allowed? I had begun to think I really wanted to. I wanted to confirm and bear witness to Edwards' malevolence, to describe the brief terror to which he had subjected me, to support all the forensic evidence with my account of the trauma of his attack on me, to ensure there was no doubt that the attack had been violent, more than just a common assault. I wanted to tell my story. But Brad could only say that they were about ninety per cent sure my evidence would be allowed, and would not know for sure until later.

He went on to tell me that, once a judge had been assigned to the trial itself, there would be regular case management meetings by video link with Edwards from Hakea Prison. These would be needed to deal with all the various applications and orders that would be presented by the prosecution and the defence in the lead-up to the trial. He asked me whether I wanted him to brief me after each of these appearances. Wanting to keep up with everything, and being so far away, I said yes.

There was no other news, but Brad reiterated that the media might well become more active now that the judge had granted the prosecution's request for a judge-only trial. They might perhaps be interested in the latest applications, he said, including the request for my evidence to be admitted, since yesterday's court hearing was the first time the public had heard of a 'propensity' matter that was considered relevant to the current charges but separate from them. They might start digging. Again, he asked me to contact him if I was approached. Although I noted this information, I was by now less concerned by this possibility. I was starting to understand that, unlike those more immediately associated with the trial in the West, I was very much anonymous, and certainly of no interest to the local media. I doubted anyone would find me.

After Brad's call, I started thinking more about the news of the past few days. Having seen again the tight, grim faces of Sarah's and Ciara's parents splashed all over the media, I wondered how they were dealing with the news of this 'propensity' evidence, with the knowledge that Edwards had attacked before and that it had been dismissed as a 'common assault'. The anger, frustration and despair that I had first felt in the immediate aftermath of the attack was now spreading to encompass the entire long-running investigation and legal proceedings. I thought of the other people who had been hounded as suspects over the past two decades, of the millions of dollars of public money that had been spent without a result. Like many others before me, I too was starting to question the approach of the Macro Task Force.

Becoming obsessed now, I searched online for the location in the southern Perth suburb of Wellard where the body of Jane Rimmer had been found. Then I searched for the spot in remote Eglinton where Ciara Glennon's body had been discovered. What connected them? Zooming in on the satellite map, it seemed so obvious. The bodies of each of these beautiful young women had been discarded in isolated spots close to overhead power and telephone lines. Had those lines been there in the mid-1990s? Had the Macro Task Force followed up on this connection, investigating any Western Power and Telstra employees who had a criminal record? I knew from media reports that the police were in possession of security-camera footage of Jane Rimmer standing outside the Continental Hotel in Claremont on the night she disappeared; it had only been released years after the murders. The only unidentified person in that video bears a resemblance to Bradley Edwards. Had the task force missed some vital links?

As the day progressed, my anxiety levels skyrocketed. I also felt so, so sad. Had the families of the murdered women read *The Devil's Garden*? Had they noticed the similarities in the body disposal sites? Did they, like me, believe that the body of Sarah Spiers had probably been left in an isolated location near some overhead power and telephone lines – a spot that would be very familiar to Telstra field technicians? Were the police, in their continuing investigations, still following these links, in their efforts to locate Sarah's body? There were so many unanswered questions; the path ahead was so unclear. There would be no sleep again for me that night.

6

As November progressed, the weather warmed and my daily walks with Maisie got longer. Following one of our regular routes, we would end up at the local dog park, where I would let her off the lead so she could gleefully roll over and over on the grass and then play with her friend Nimh the collie, chasing each other around the park until they were both exhausted. On the morning of Edwards' first scheduled case management meeting, we had just waved goodbye to Nimh and I was reattaching Maisie's lead when a text arrived telling me that Edwards had just appeared in the Supreme Court by video link from Hakea Prison. When we got home, I searched online for the news.

It was reported that Supreme Court Justice Stephen Hall would be presiding over the trial. A well-respected judge, he had previously presided over several other high-profile cases in Western Australia. The defence case would likely include evidence from alibi witnesses and overseas experts. Edwards' lawyer Paul Yovich had told the court that it would be 'unfair' to his client if the trial started the following May, because the magnitude of the case meant that the defence team would not be ready; it had already taken some time for them to find an appropriate DNA expert to testify at the trial. He also suggested that they might seek to have each of the charges heard separately.

Justice Hall had responded that he had now scheduled regular case management meetings and would not consider any delay to the trial's start date at this stage. Prosecutors were now apparently saying that their case would run for approximately eight months, plus at least a month for the defence case. Carmel Barbagallo was still intending to make an application for propensity evidence to be heard.

I hoped that would happen soon. I wanted to know what, if anything, would be expected of me. Would I be an observer or a participant in this mammoth upcoming trial?

* * *

Kate and her family arrived for Christmas 2018. I remember driving back with her from a busy and entertaining morning at the park with the three little cousins all together. The littlies were in the back, tired out and fractious from the morning's activity. They were so loud that I barely heard the phone ringing. Expecting a call from a friend regarding some Christmas arrangements, I answered, growling at the kids to keep the noise down. It was Brad Hollingsworth. He asked whether it was a good time to update me on the previous day's pre-trial hearing. I realised that I had, for a little while, forgotten about Bradley Edwards. I requested that he call back later, explaining that I was preoccupied with family but that I was of course interested as the court proceedings didn't appear in the local news.

It was late afternoon when he called back. It seemed that things were moving forward with increasing speed. Edwards had appeared at the hearing by video link, with members of the Spiers and Glennon families watching from the public gallery. It was revealed that DNA and fibre evidence would form a key part of the prosecution's evidence and that, in relation to this, they would obtain reports from PathWest and ChemCentre in Western Australia, and from UK forensics company Cellmark. The prosecutors also intended to present as evidence some 'stories of interest' that had been written and downloaded by Edwards. Further, they were seeking to obtain his medical records and information from Telstra including his employment records, personal leave dates and vehicle use. Prosecutor Carmel Barbagallo stated that there would need to be a number of pre-trial hearings to deal with the admissibility of evidence, including propensity evidence. The defence team had now been provided with tens of thousands of pages of DNA, hair and fibre evidence and some of the stories taken from various electronic devices seized from Edwards' home after his arrest.

Mr Yovich suggested that the defence team might well object to the admissibility of some of this evidence, and reiterated that, given the sheer amount of evidence, it would not be feasible to start the trial in May. It had therefore now been set to begin on 1 July and was likely to run for nine months.

Brad explained that the prosecution's request to admit my evidence as propensity evidence would be made at the next pre-trial hearing, which was scheduled for February the following year, so I should know then whether I would be required to attend court. I wondered whether that hearing would be open to the public and to the media, whether my identity would then no longer be private.

As I thanked Brad for the update and put the phone down, I wondered just where this journey was heading – for me, for the families of Sarah, Jane and Ciara, for the other living victims, and even for Edwards – and knew that a part of me was tied inextricably to what was happening in the West.

7

It was a few weeks later, one evening in early February 2019, that Brad Hollingsworth called to update me on the second case management meeting. I could hear that he again sounded tired, and I realised it was close of business time in Perth and he had no doubt had an exceptionally long day. I thought that I was probably one of several potential witnesses he was keeping informed as best he could as events transpired.

The meeting had been held in the Supreme Court, with Edwards again appearing by video link. The prosecution had nearly finished disclosing its DNA evidence, and the defence had reiterated its intention to call its own DNA and other experts to testify during the trial itself. Further forensic work was still being conducted on the clothes that Ciara Glennon had been wearing on the night she'd disappeared, and on a vehicle that Edwards had been driving at the time.

Importantly, the defence team had stated that it definitely wanted two of the charges to be heard separately from the main trial. These were the 1988 sexual assault in Huntingdale, which had preceded the attack on me, and the 1995 rape in Karrakatta Cemetery, which had preceded the three murders. The prosecution was still hoping to include propensity evidence at the murder trial, which would surely include these two other assaults if they were proven.

All of the proposed applications for evidence would be presented to Justice Hall at a pre-trial hearing, at which Edwards would appear in person. The defence team had indicated that it would apply for this hearing to be partly or fully suppressed, due to the nature of the material to be discussed. Brad assured me once again that this meant my name would not be made public, and I was grateful. I was beginning to understand just how complicated this trial was going to be, and how difficult it would be for the judge to establish the legality and relevance of all the presenting evidence. I continued to wonder just what part I would be required to play.

* * *

In mid-February, my brother John and his wife Brenda came from northern New South Wales to spend a week with us. Having lived apart for many years and been busy with work and families, we spent precious days catching up on family news and just enjoying each other's company. As we shopped, shared the preparations for our meals, walked the dog, took a leisurely drive to the top of Kunanyi (Mount Wellington), visited my daughter Martha and her family, I was reminded of what life had felt like before Edwards was arrested. For a while, my focus shifted back to stories of our own families' lives, their achievements, their trials and tribulations, their hopes, their plans and their dreams. But the truth was that the trial was never far from my mind.

The day before they were due to leave, we were enjoying our morning coffee and planning our day when I asked John if he wanted to read what I had written so far about my experience with the Claremont trial. He'd told me he was keen to understand more about my journey, so I passed him my laptop. He read in silence, occasionally frowning. After a while he closed the laptop, came over to me, put his arms around me and held me close. Words were unnecessary.

My phone broke the silence, and I moved away to answer it. Unexpectedly, and as if by telepathy, it was Brad Hollingsworth. His voice sounded lighter than it had during the previous call, and I could sense anticipation and some excitement as he relayed that things were now moving more quickly, that the next day's pre-trial hearing would be significant in many ways, and that he hoped I was coping okay now that the trial itself was getting closer, becoming more real. He wanted to update me on a few things before the hearing, he said, explaining that they related to legal arguments regarding the admission of evidence.

The defence intended to ask for certain witnesses not to be permitted to attend court for the pre-trial hearings, because their evidence was critical to what would be discussed. These included Edwards' other living victims. Brad explained that the media would be free to report on what was presented in court, and that once they heard of Edwards' previous conviction for his attack on me, it would be big news. He reiterated that my name would be suppressed, and told me not to be concerned if some of the conclusions drawn by the media after the hearing were incorrect, as they would not be in possession of all the factual evidence until the trial. Significantly, he also said that the defence team's earlier request to have the two lesser charges heard separately might affect the admissibility of my evidence, given that Edwards' attack on me had occurred between those two assaults.

The hearing was expected to run for at least two days, Brad said, and Justice Hall might then take up to a month to decide on the admissibility of the evidence. So there would be more weeks of waiting. Brad's final words to me in that conversation were heartening. The families of Sarah Spiers, Jane Rimmer and Ciara Glennon had been informed that I was willing to travel to Western Australia to give evidence, and they had expressed their thanks.

I took John and Brenda to the airport the next afternoon. As we said our goodbyes, they offered to come back later in the year to house-and-dog–sit for us if I was called to testify at the trial. It was a big relief to me to know that, if Tim felt well enough at the time, he would be able to accompany me to Perth and we would not have to rush to get back to Maisie or the house. We would be able to catch up with family and friends together, and he would be there to support me.

Driving home from the airport, I remembered that I was expecting to receive another call from Brad Hollingsworth that evening at around eight pm Hobart time, to fill me in on the day's pre-trial hearing, so I was surprised when he rang just as I pulled into the driveway. He explained that, because of a dispute regarding some new evidence, Carmel Barbagallo had requested that the hearing be adjourned until the following Monday. He also said that the day's therefore very short proceedings would be all over the WA news, so I could search online for more details if I wished. He would ring me again on Monday after the adjourned hearing.

The media did not disappoint. It reported that the day's proceedings had lasted less than an hour, and had been interrupted in the first few seconds by a woman's screams from the public gallery: 'Edwards, evil dog! Rot in hell with Satan! You're a dog, Edwards, a dog! Evil Satan, burn in hell!' Edwards had apparently not reacted to the outburst, and the woman had quickly been escorted from the courtroom.

Carmel Barbagallo had then requested more time to put together a schedule of new evidence relevant to the questions of admissibility. This evidence included witness statements, a six-hour police interview, and some graphic pornography that she described as 'extreme'. Mr Yovich had challenged some of the evidence, and maintained that Justice Hall did not need to view the material. Justice Hall had responded that he would view the material, but would direct himself to disregard it at the trial if it was deemed inadmissible.

Justice Hall had also explained to the court that there were eight categories of potentially admissible evidence for consideration: evidence relating to the Huntingdale prowler offences, evidence relating to the Huntingdale offences, women's clothing evidence, Hollywood Hospital evidence, Telstra living witness evidence, Karrakatta offences evidence, evidence relating to the three murder charges, and pornography-related evidence.

I wondered whether other people, like me, were beginning to put the story together, starting to see the development of a killer, the escalating pattern of depraved and violent behaviour that had eventually led, it would seem, to murder. But then, if Edwards was indeed guilty of the murders of three young women in Claremont in the 1990s, why had he stopped? Perhaps that would become clear as the story unfolded.

It felt to me as though the process of bringing Edwards to trial was jump-starting and then stalling, repeatedly. Feeling my own anxiety levels steadily rising, I wondered how the families of the murdered young women were coping. The other two women who had been attacked would be close to fifty years old by now, I realised, perhaps with families of their own. How were they feeling?

8

I can still recall the confusion and concern that surrounded what happened on the day of that scheduled pre-trial hearing – Monday 18 February 2019. I also remember the feeling of disconnection I had experienced, being so far away. Sometimes it was as if I was in two places at once: in Hobart, there were no local media reports on the trial, and nobody spoke of the Claremont serial killer; in Perth, it dominated the media, and the whole community was affected by what was happening. And I was a part of it, but, at the same time, far away, excluded.

The previous few weeks had been very busy for me, first with John and Brenda's visit and then with our friend Vikki moving house. I had been helping her with the move, and on that Monday, we had just finished emptying the last of the kitchen boxes and were resting with a well-earned cuppa when I was reminded once again that I was linked inextricably to what was occurring in the West. A text message arrived from my daughter Jo in Darwin: 'Edwards has stabbed himself.'

Stunned, I searched online for the WA news, and it was everywhere – although exactly what had happened was not clear: 'hearing delayed' ... 'attacked in the shower block at Hakea Prison at 8.30 am' ... 'stab wound to the ear' ... 'pencil found nearby' ... 'twenty-one other prisoners in the unit' ... 'not life-threatening'. Over the next few hours, as the reporting intensifed, it was accompanied by photos of Edwards on a stretcher being taken to Perth's Fiona Stanley Hospital, a bandage covering his right ear.

There was much speculation about exactly how Edwards had come to be injured. A statement from the state's corrective services commissioner Tony Hassall laid out the basic facts of the incident: Edwards had gone for a shower when the unit had been unlocked at 7.30 am, and had been found injured in the shower block about twenty minutes later. Corrective services minister Fran Logan initially reported that Edwards had been attacked by another prisoner in the shower block, but later clarified that he had no indication of how the injury had occurred. Attorney-General John Quigley weighed in, saying he was concerned about the incident and about the effect that any delay to the trial would have on the victims' families. He emphasised the need to keep Edwards secure and in good health to face trial without further postponements.

It felt as though the rug had suddenly been pulled from under everyone's feet. Just as everyone had been all psyched up to face the first public revelations of the case against a man accused of multiple brutal murders, the process had once again come to a grinding halt.

As the day progressed, with no real further information, my thoughts jumped from once scenario to another. How injured was he? Was he suicidal – or just calculating? Maybe his mental state would break down completely? Would this delay the hearing for any length of time? Given his notoriety and the importance to the entire Western Australian community that justice was finally served for these horrific crimes, it was unfathomable to me that Edwards was not in twenty-four-hour isolation, on safety watch.

As I processed the news further, I became convinced that Edwards had harmed himself. He had been in prison for more than two years – if another prisoner had wanted to injure him, it surely would have happened sooner and the injury would have been far more serious. I thought that he was most likely trying to delay the inevitable, and maybe even gain some sympathy. But sympathy from whom? From the public, who were becoming increasingly horrified as more details of his alleged crimes were unveiled? From his family? Was there anyone left who still supported him, cared for him?

When Brad Hollingsworth called – much earlier in the day than either of us had anticipated – I told him I'd found the news disturbing, the delay frustrating, and he agreed and said he was sorry but there was going to be a bit more waiting before I would hear whether my evidence would be accepted. He stressed that Edwards' injury was not serious, and said that the hearing would likely go ahead the following morning.

Like me, Brad thought the injury had been self-inflicted. He said that Edwards had known that the previous week's hearing would be rescheduled, which was why he had appeared so calm in court that day. But on that Monday morning the reality of what was happening, perhaps exacerbated by the media reporting over the weekend, might have influenced him to try to delay things. I think we both mentally added, '... or perhaps even try to kill himself,' but that thought remained unspoken because, for both of us and almost certainly for the other living victims and the families of the murdered women, it was the last thing anyone wanted to happen. If Edwards was indeed guilty, he needed to face justice.

I heard later from a friend who knew someone in Hakea Prison that word around the prison was that Edwards had inflicted the wound on himself.

* * *

As Brad had predicted, that pre-trial hearing did go ahead the day after Edwards' injury. It ran for two days, and and was even more eventful than anticipated.

The *West Australian* reported on the proceedings live from the courtroom, and I followed its coverage online from late morning Hobart time. I wanted to know what the prosecution was putting forward, what the defence was arguing against and – increasingly important to me as the trial date grew closer – just where I fitted in. I was happy that things appeared to be moving forward at last.

First, Carmel Barbagallo presented an overview of the evidence that the prosecution wished to present at the trial, briefly detailing the various categories that it had been divided into. Some of these categories were then argued against by the defence. As each category was reported, and more horrific details of Edwards' alleged behaviour revealed, the story became more complicated. However, by the time Justice Hall retired to study the arguments, a clear and terrible picture had begun to emerge: that of the development of a socially awkward teenager into a sadistic killer.

The first category of evidence outlined by the prosecution related to the 'Huntingdale prowler' allegations. In January 1988, it had been reported in the media that a prowler was lurking around Huntingdale, stealing women's underwear from clotheslines. One evening, a man wearing a silk kimono had broken into a woman's house, and that same man was apparently later seen trying to open the rear sliding door of another house, both in Huntingdale. Finger and palm prints had been taken from the latter scene. The following month, again in Huntingdale, a man had broken into a house where an eighteen-year-old woman had been asleep, lying on her stomach. He had straddled her from behind and, when she woke, attempted to push a cloth into her mouth. She'd struggled, and her attacker had fled, leaving behind a white silk kimono and a pair of knotted black stockings. Many years later, that kimono had been found to contain Edwards' DNA. The prosecution maintained that he was the Huntingdale prowler, and that his actions at that time clearly demonstrated the beginnings of a pattern of sexually motivated violent and deviant behaviour. They proposed to present related evidence of a fetish for collecting and wearing women's underwear, bizarrely modifying women's clothes, and possessing homemade sex toys. The defence argued strenuously that this evidence should not be admissible, as it had no relevance to the murdering of three young women elsewhere in Perth almost a decade later.

The second category of evidence proposed by the prosecution related to the Hollywood Hospital attack on me in 1990. It was outlined to the court that Edwards had attacked me from behind, tried to stuff something into my mouth and attempted to drag me into the toilet. I had kicked him and broken free, a security guard had been called, and Edwards had been held until police had arrived. They'd found cable ties in his pocket. Edwards had apologised and pleaded guilty to common assault, and had received two years probation.

In response to the prosecution's outlining of this incident, defence barrister Mr Yovich pointed out that Edwards had been told by his girlfriend the day before the incident that she had been unfaithful to him, that he had taken exception to 'a curt comment' that had been made, and that he had apologised for his actions.

A 'curt comment'? Casting my mind back to the information I had given Katy and Brendan, it occurred to me that my statement had probably already been provided to the defence. Rereading my own copy, I saw that I had made mention of being busy when Edwards had spoken to me in my office, so focused on my work that I had merely nodded and grunted my assent when he'd asked to use the toilet. Perhaps it was this that his defence had seized on, interpreting my nod and grunt as 'curt' to explain his reaction, his anger, his attack on me – suggesting some provocation for his seemingly inexplicable actions.

And his 'apology'? His mumbled repeating of 'I'm sorry, I'm sorry, I'm sorry' immediately upon my breaking free from his hold was hardly an apology – more a frantic realisation that I had escaped, and that he was likely to be held accountable for what he'd just done. Or perhaps Mr Yovich was referring to the apology from the Telecom manager for the 'unfortunate incident', during that meeting in the days following the attack?

Later, as I read the various media reports about 'the Hollywood Hospital evidence', I felt a familiar sense of despair. I had told the Telecom manager in that meeting that Edwards' behaviour had not been normal, had not been a typical response to experiencing relationship problems. If only he had listened. If only the police had recognised Edwards' actions at the time as strange, unusual, dangerous, as deserving of more investigation. Surely they would have noted that he lived in Huntingdale, the scene of a night-time prowler and attacker only a year or two earlier? It had now become clear that they'd even had fingerprints on file to compare. If only they had spoken to me further, had listened to what I was saying. But no-one had. They'd dismissed me. No-one had followed it up. They'd missed a chance.

In the next category, referred to as the Karrakatta evidence, the prosecution revealed details about an attack made on a seventeen-year-old woman as she was walking home alone in Claremont in February 1995. Her attacker had grabbed her from behind, thrown her to the ground, placed a hood over her head and bound her hands with a knotted cord. He'd then pushed her into his car and driven her to nearby Karrakatta Cemetery, where he'd raped her twice and left her bound and naked from the waist down. She'd managed to make her way to nearby Hollywood Hospital, where swab samples had been taken and the police called. According to the prosecution, there were clear similarities in behaviour between the Huntingdale assault, the Hollywood Hospital attack on me, and the Karrakatta Cemetery rape. In each case the victim had been attacked from behind with no warning, and a gag or hood had been used to silence them. Ms Barbagallo maintained that, together, the offences demonstrated a developing modus operandi – one that had ultimately led to murder. Mr Yovich argued that the circumstances in each situation were quite different, in that one had involved someone in bed, one had occurred in broad daylight in a workplace, and one had happened on a street late at night.

Ms Barbagallo then went on to outline what she described as the Telstra living witnesses' evidence. This proposed evidence related to a series of incidents in the mid-1990s in which a man in a car with a Telecom or Telstra logo (Telecom was renamed Telstra in 1995) had been seen driving around the suburbs of Claremont and Cottesloe, offering young women lifts. He'd told one woman he was looking for 'damsels in distress', had given another woman a lift and, after he'd dropped her off, had followed her and tried to kiss her. Someone else had reported a man in a white car with a Telstra logo stopping and staring at two women waiting for a taxi, before driving off. Ms Barbagallo alleged that the man driving these vehicles was Edwards, and that his behaviour in these cases had been similar to that displayed in the Huntingdale incidents and the Claremont murders, showing a clear tendency to prowl in familiar areas to seize on opportunities to fulfil his fantasies. Mr Yovich disagreed, saying that the incidents were all very different.

The next category of proposed evidence was referred to as the Claremont series. This related directly to the disappearances and murders of the young women from Claremont that had occurred between January 1996 and March 1997.

Eighteen-year-old legal secretary Sarah Spiers had been the first to disappear. Having called a taxi from a payphone in Claremont in the early hours of 27 January 1996 after a night out with friends, when the taxi had arrived, she was gone. A resident six kilometres away in Mosman Park had reportedly heard 'bloodcurdling screams' an hour later. He'd looked out of his window and seen a car with the distinctive curved brakelights of a 1992 Toyota Camry – the same model of car that Edwards was driving at the time.

Later that year, just after midnight on 6 June, twenty-three-year-old childcare worker Jane Rimmer had declined a lift home with friends from Club Bayview in Claremont. Later that night, residents in the southern suburb of Wellard had reportedly heard a 'loud, high-pitched scream' that had stopped abruptly and been followed by silence. Jane's remains were found in Wellard fifty-five days later by a woman out bushwalking. Two months later, a Telstra knife was found in a Telstra box in the area. Although it was standard issue for Telstra technicians at the time, the knife had not been used for work in that area. After Edwards' arrest, detectives found two similar knives in his toolbox, and fibres from Jane's hair were later found to match fibres found in a Telstra car issued to Edwards.

The following year, on the evening of 14 March 1997, twenty-seven-year-old lawyer Ciara Glennon had been out with friends in Claremont and was last seen talking with the occupant of a late-model Holden Commodore at traffic lights on Stirling Highway. Edwards had been due at a friend's house in Dawesville, south of Perth, that night, but he did not arrive until midmorning the following day, saying he'd been with his (first) wife, trying to reconcile. Ms Barbagallo told the court that this was a lie, and that Edwards had no explanation for being so late. Eighteen days later, Ciara's remains were found in remote Eglinton, north of Perth, by a walker. DNA found beneath her fingernails was later matched with Edwards'; it also matched swabs taken from the Karrakatta rape victim and semen samples found on the kimono left at the scene of the Huntingdale assault. Fibres taken from Ciara's hair also matched fibres found in the Holden Commodore Edwards was driving for Telstra at the time.

In total, the prosecution intended to present a sixty-thousand-page DNA report relating to the Claremont evidence. Although Mr Yovich agreed that DNA evidence would be central to his client's trial, he stated that the defence team would be calling on its own experts to challenge the prosecution's DNA evidence, suggesting that issues of contamination or other 'innocent' contact may be relevant to the defence's case.

Pornography was the fifth and final category of evidence presented for consideration by the prosecution. Ms Barbagallo made mention of Edwards' collection of extreme, graphic, hardcore pornography and violent erotic stories. She said that much of this material indicated an obsessive interest in the abduction, imprisonment and violent rape of women rendered helpless by their captor, and that 'no description ... adequately reflects what was in the material'. She maintained that Edwards was the author of several detailed stories that bore striking similarities to the crimes he was alleged to have committed. She also emphasised the apparent impact of Edwards' emotional state on his behaviour, stating that each of the alleged offences and the proven Hollywood Hospital attack had occurred when Edwards had been experiencing significant relationship difficulties. According to the prosecution, the breakdown of Edwards' most recent relationship had coincided with increased use of pornographic material.

In summary, the prosecution team was requesting that Justice Hall admit all the proposed evidence, as they believed it was inextricably linked and showed common themes that, once proven in court, would demonstrate the escalation of a socially awkward teenager with a penchant for women's underwear to a violent serial killer motivated by sexual gratification and triggered by emotional distress. The defence, on the other hand, was arguing that the various offences were each very different, that the Huntingdale allegations were irrelevant to the murders and should be heard separately, that the motivations for the murders might not have been sexual, and that the DNA evidence was arguable.

As I read the prosecution's account of Edwards' apparent pre-occupation with various unusual and in some cases somewhat depraved sexual activities – including reading and writing violent erotic stories, collecting and wearing women's clothing, wearing women's underwear with holes cut out, and masturbating into ziplock bags – I wondered whether his family had been aware of this bizarre and concerning behaviour. If not, it seemed he'd been living a parallel secret life alongside maintaining his 'normal' public persona.

Walking with Maisie the day after the hearing finished, trying to clear my head, I could feel that I was still totally immersed in this terrible story. Usually our walks are my relaxation – I'm aware of my surroundings, the weather, the birds, the hum of traffic in the background. But not that day. After reading and rereading the media reports of the court proceedings, I was once again engulfed by the feelings that had overwhelmed me after the attack: the fear, the hypervigilance, the anger. Realising the extent of the depravity and violence that was emerging as events were gradually being pieced together, I could feel a little of the terror that must have been felt by the victims and the despair of their families, and I was filled with anxiety and sorrow.

9

On 20 March 2019, Justice Hall handed down his decisions on the admissibility of the prosecution's propensity evidence, and on the defence's application to have the matters heard in two separate trials. Edwards appeared by video link, and members of the victims' families were in the courtroom. Unlike the previous hearing, the proceedings were not streamed live, but the news reports were comprehensive and almost instantaneous once the hearing was over. I was astounded to read that there would be 580 witnesses appearing for the prosecution, and I wondered about the magnitude of the work involved in collecting, collating and presenting so much evidence.

There would be one trial only. The Huntingdale evidence, which included the sightings of a man breaking into houses and stealing and wearing women's clothing, would not be admissible in relation to the three murder allegations. Justice Hall also ruled that the extreme pornography was not sufficiently relevant to the trial to be included. All the other evidence, including that relating to the Huntingdale assault, the Hollywood Hospital attack, the Karrakatta rape and the Telstra living witnesses, were admissible to all the charges. It appeared that I would be one of the 580 witnesses required to give evidence.

I'd had little time to think about the implications of this development for me, when Brad Hollingsworth called. He wanted to confirm that I was following the proceedings, and that I was aware that this meant that I would now definitely be required to give evidence. Because the prosecution's vast body of evidence was to be presented in chronological order, he anticipated that the Hollywood Hospital evidence would be presented around the end of August or beginning of September, and he explained that Carmel Barbagallo would ideally like to meet with me prior to my appearance to discuss the evidence and the procedure. I told him that Tim and I were intending to come to Perth for a month, to make it easier to attend all the relevant trial proceedings, and that we would take the opportunity to visit and stay with friends and family. Brad seemed happy with this arrangement, which we agreed to firm up in the next month or so.

In the days following the March hearing, further media reports from the West revealed more bits of the huge jigsaw that the prosecution was trying to piece together in its mammoth undertaking to prove Bradley Edwards guilty of the Claremont killings. Reports on 21 March 2019 stated that Edwards had been ordered to attend a year-long, sex-offenders treatment program more than five years before the Claremont killings. This puzzled me. Had there been another charge in or around 1990? Had he committed another offence that had prompted the court to order treatment for sex offending? Reading further, it became clear that he had been placed in the program after he had attacked me. This was the first I had heard of this, and none of it made any sense to me. At the time of the attack, I had been very much aware that I'd been very violently attacked, that I'd been at risk of rape, or worse. I'd been told there wasn't enough evidence to confirm this, that he'd never done anything like it before, that he'd 'just snapped', that it had been 'a one-off'. No-one had mentioned sexual assault. If the police had in fact understood that the attack on me had been sexually motivated – given the cable ties, the bruising around my neck, the cloth over my mouth and the location – surely this should have warranted a more serious charge than common assault? Surely Telecom should have been more concerned at the behaviour of this employee? *I* had known it was serious. And it now seemed that the magistrate who had dealt with Edwards had also known it was serious. So why had he only been charged with common assault? And furthermore, if he had been ordered to attend a sex-offenders program, then surely his name would have been on a list of sexual offenders in the area when the police were investigating the murders?

I wondered then whether Edwards' parents and brother had even known at the time of the Hollywood Hospital attack, of the charge, of the program? Media reports about his family were still relatively sparse. They were obviously and quite understandably keeping a low profile. Apparently, his parents and brother visited him in jail. His brother had publicly maintained his sibling's innocence, saying that the trial would prove he was not responsible for the crimes of which he was accused. Maybe the Hollywood Hospital attack had been so downplayed by Edwards, by his employer, by the police and even by the court system that his family had seen it merely as a one-off lapse of control, understandable to them within the context of his stress levels and relationship difficulties at the time. Something minor, easily forgotten.

I imagined, though, that the DNA evidence, the links with the Huntingdale crimes and the extreme pornography must, by now, be ringing some alarm bells. I was sure that everyone in Edwards' family and social network would be trying to make sense of the events of the past two years, questioning themselves, their knowledge of their son, brother, friend. Whether they were in denial or simply hoping against hope, the day of reckoning was now approaching. Details revealed at the last pre-trial hearing suggested that much of the evidence presented at the trial would be detailed, graphic and horrendous. If Edwards was found guilty, I could not begin to imagine how his family would be able to process what would no longer be allegations, but facts.

More doubts were now also being raised about the Macro Task Force investigation. Media articles asked whether the Telstra prowler reports had been properly investigated at the time, or whether investigators had been so totally preoccupied with other potential leads, so narrowly focused, that they'd missed vital clues that could have solved the mystery much sooner. Other reports referred to the Hollywood Hospital assault, questioning how Edwards had kept his job after the attack, and wondering whether Telstra had been aware of the incident.

On 26 March, the *West Australian* reported what it referred to as a 'bombshell twist' in the case against Edwards. Former police commissioner Karl O'Callaghan told of a witness statement relating to a Telstra vehicle seen in the vicinity of the 1995 abduction and rape of the young woman in Karrakatta Cemetery, a year before the murders. I wondered whether this clue had been followed up. Further links to Telstra also emerged, with O'Callaghan stating that in 2004, the police had had evidence of a man in a Telstra vehicle stalking young women in the Claremont area. Again, had this been followed up? Had anyone checked the criminal records of Telstra workers? As these facts were emerging, I could only begin to imagine the distress that the families of the victims must be feeling, the questions they, like me, must be asking.

On 1 April, retired detective sergeant Tony Potts rebutted what he referred to as 'ignorant' and 'ill-timed' public comments about the Macro Task Force investigation. Potts had been part of the task force management team between 1996 and 2000, and had overseen its media strategy. He maintained that all Telstra links had been followed up at the time, leading to no outcome. Telstra officials declined to comment, saying that the matter was before the courts.

When I was attacked at Hollywood Hospital in 1990, both the WA police and Telecom had dismissed the incident as 'minor', a 'one-off', 'out of character' and 'explainable' given my assailant's 'relationship problems'. Nearly three decades later, it was becoming clear to everyone that it was in fact none of those things.

* * *

By Tim's birthday at the end of March, I was feeling unwell. I was anxious, stressed, physically exhausted, and so unlike my normal self – myself before the arrest of Bradley Edwards more than two years ago, far away on the other side of the continent. I felt torn in half, trying to maintain my daily life around me, but at the same time connected to the events going on in the West. I felt a sense of responsibility, of attachment, that I couldn't verbalise. I didn't want it but I couldn't shake it off. I didn't feel like writing, I didn't feel like doing anything, really. As I listened to Tim chatting away to one of his birthday callers, I thought I would just organise a nice takeaway for our dinner. I didn't have the energy to cook or to dine out; I hadn't even taken Maisie for a walk. The court proceedings of the previous month or so had dominated my life, I was physically and emotionally depleted, and my thoughts were far away, focused on the events happening on the other side of the country.

In mid-April I received a phone call from a detective sergeant from Western Australia Police. His name was Aaron and he was associated with the Macro Task Force and the DPP. I missed his exact connections, but he seemed to know that Tim and I were planning to be in Perth for a while around the time of my court appearance. He informed me that he was required to personally present me with a summons to attend court for the trial of Bradley Edwards, which would begin on 22 July, and asked whether I would be home the following Tuesday. He would be flying from Melbourne, he said, and would be able to answer any questions I may have about my court appearance. He sounded friendly, with a strong voice that emanated confidence. We agreed on a time to meet, and I felt pleased that the process was clearly now moving forward.

After much consideration, I had by now decided that I definitely wanted to give my evidence in court, not by video link. I thought that the impact would be more powerful for the prosecution, and that the families of the murdered women and the other living victims would feel more supported if I was able to tell in person what happened all those years ago. I was also hoping that the process would represent some sort of closure for me – of finally facing Edwards myself, relaying the attack in detail, finally being heard. When I told Brad Hollingsworth of my decision, he told me that I could have a support person come to court with me on the day I gave my evidence, if I wished. Considering this, I felt that the experience would be stressful enough without the added responsibility of having to negotiate the environment and the protocol, so I contacted Katy, the detective who had maintained contact with me throughout the entire process. She understood my request and agreed that, although she would not be able to come into the courtroom with me, she would pick me up from wherever I was staying, drive me to court and wait outside the courtroom until I'd finished giving evidence so that she could drive me back home again.

* * *

Winter finally snuck into Hobart after an unusually long and humid summer. On the day Aaron was due to come, the predicted maximum temperature was just fourteen degrees and I'm not sure we even reached it. It was bitterly cold at four am when I awoke to the dog trying to burrow her way under the bedcovers. After breakfast I pulled on a coat for the first time since the previous November and walked her to the park. As I felt the icy, needle-like shards of light rain blowing down from the mountain, I wished I'd worn my beanie.

Aaron arrived midmorning. He explained that he worked with the Macro prosecution team, and he was very focused on ensuring that I understood the summons to attend court. I was a little disappointed that he didn't seem interested in my story – I realised of course that mine was one of many such subpoenas that he would be serving but, because of my previous experience of feeling that the WA police had downplayed, even trivialised, the attack on me, I was very sensitive to their current attitudes and opinions. He informed me that, within a few hours of our visit, he would be flying back to Melbourne where he and some colleagues would be meeting with other witnesses, including DNA experts. After a brief discussion, he enquired as to a good place to eat in town and was on his way.

I sat down to study the summons in more detail. As expected, it stated that I might be required to attend court on one or more consecutive days, and that the DPP would be in touch with me to arrange a pre-trial conference to discuss the evidence I was legally able to give at the trial, the courtroom set-up, procedure and etiquette and any questions I might have. I found myself looking forward to this meeting with anticipation and a little trepidation.

10

At the beginning of May I travelled to Darwin for four days. My youngest daughter Jo had recently begun a three-year postdoctoral contract with Charles Darwin University, and I'd decided to take a brief sojourn from Hobart's cold weather and pay a surprise visit for my granddaughter's third birthday.

It was my first time in Darwin, and it was like being in another world – a tropical world of heat, humidity, insects, lethargy and beer. It was strange, stepping out of the terminal into the blistering heat. This little granddaughter had been a big part of our lives since the day she was born, and I was missing her so much. The surprise and pleasure on her face when I turned up, unexpected, unannounced, to pick her up from day care was priceless, something I will never forget.

My visit was an excuse for my daughter to deviate from the mundane routine of daily life. She took a few days off work and we celebrated her birthday as well. Far from Hobart, far from Perth and the trial proceedings, as we swam in the gorges and called for jumping crocodiles to entertain us on winding streams and rivers in the wetlands, our only focus was on keeping cool. It was so good to just spend some time with them, to forget about what was happening in the West, and I returned to Hobart full and happy.

* * *

There was another case management meeting on 7 June. When Brad Hollingsworth called me late that afternoon, he sounded exhausted, excited, determined and concerned all at once, and I tried to focus on his words as he attempted to update me on the morning's proceedings.

The biggest news was that the trial was going to be delayed again. This time it was due to the processing of 'new and significant fibre evidence' that was still being analysed by prosecution experts. Their reports would not be finalised until the end of June, and the defence claimed that their own experts would then need some months to examine the reports and prepare their reply. I read later that the fibres were associated with Telstra uniform trousers worn by Telstra technicians during the time of the murders. Additional evidence to be presented related to fibres taken from a Telstra vehicle driven by Edwards in the 1990s. This evidence was apparently now central to the case. Further evidence revealed in court detailed a report from 2014 linking fibres found on the body of Ciara Glennon with fibres found on the teenage victim raped in Karrakatta Cemetery in 1995. It had been reported by the media at that time that this evidence had shown that the same person was responsible for both attacks, but the police would not comment. At that time, they had not yet known the attacker's identity.

Brad said that, although he understood the delay was difficult, the reality was the prosecution team was very tired from the pace of work required to prepare all the evidence so far, they were still interviewing witnesses and they needed more time to, firstly, finish preparing what would ultimately be a massive body of evidence and, secondly, catch their breath before what looked likely to be an exhausting nine-month trial, the likes of which Perth had never seen.

I asked how the families of the victims were coping with the delay, and he said that they were understandably disappointed but at the same time very cognisant of the fact that there would only be one opportunity to try to convict Edwards, and that it must be done as effectively as possible. He mentioned that one of the key witnesses had been in court that morning and she'd appeared upset and left abruptly when the delay had been announced. I wondered whether she was one of Edwards' other victims, someone having trouble coping with yet another delay, yet more months added to what must surely be a traumatic journey for her.

Knowing that I had multiple arrangements to make in order to be able to attend court, Brad was apologetic for the delay, and said that the prosecution team would be as flexible and accommodating as possible regarding my court dates. He said that my appearance was now expected to be the following January or February. I explained to him then that summer in Perth was difficult for us, particularly Tim, and he asked whether Tim had a medical problem or was it just because he was Tasmanian? I smiled at this question, because most Tasmanians I know love to get away to warmer climes for a holiday. I told Brad that no, it was because Tim has MS and finds it difficult to manage the heat. I went on to explain that it was only the recent implementation of direct flights from Perth to Hobart that had prompted Tim to agree to come to Perth to support me, that he had not left the state for many years due to the fatigue associated with travel.

Brad acknowledged this, and went on to say that although the judge had seemed to understand their request for a delay, he had not been happy about the resulting impacts on both the families and the accused. Justice Hall maintained that Edwards had now been in prison for more than two-and-a-half years, and that any further delays would prejudice his right to fair treatment under the law. He would not accept the presentation of any further new evidence after a 31 June deadline without special application. Carmel Barbagallo had noted that the ruling was very unusual, but the judge was adamant. So the police were still investigating, new evidence was coming to light all the time but, in order to prevent the legal process from dragging on ad infinitum, the judge had drawn a line in the sand that hopefully would not be washed away yet again. Ending our conversation, Brad reminded me that Ms Barbagallo would be in touch before the trial, at which point we would be able to confirm dates and organise flights.

Reading the news from Western Australia later that day, I was again struck by the enormity of the prosecution's task over the next five months. It had been revealed at the hearing that the evidence currently housed on an entire floor of the office of the DPP had now been collated into an electronic database. All items were cross-referenced, marked as exhibits for tendering in court and backed up for access in case of a system failure.

***

Over the next week, I gradually informed those family and friends who would be involved in some way in supporting us to attend the trial that it looked as though we would not now be going to Perth until January. When I told my brother, who with his wife would be coming down to Hobart from northern New South Wales to house-and-dog-sit for us, to my amusement he was happy about the delay, saying that the warmer summer weather would be better for their southern sojourn. Apparently, they'd been a little concerned that September in Hobart might still be too chilly for northern New South Welshmen!

By midwinter there was snow atop Kunanyi (Mount Wellington), the beautiful backdrop to our city. The weather was very unpredictable: freezing crisp sunny periods alternated with unusually mild overcast days. It was trying hard to rain but the thick dark clouds only managed to produce a few drops here and there and most Hobartians were still hand-watering their gardens. In June the winter solstice was marked by the Dark MoFo festival, an event that had become increasingly popular over the past seven years, drawing crowds from all over the world to the island. Salamanca Square was closed to traffic and filled instead with all sorts of entertainment and local and exotic food stalls. Walking past the docks at night became an adventure, with huge red illuminated crosses dominating the skyline and towering flames from open fires flickering among the crowds. Families and groups of friends gathered to celebrate the full moon that signified the beginning of longer hours of daylight, the moving towards the summer.

***

I was missing my Perth family and my friends in the West. With uncanny timing, my eldest daughter Kate called from Perth to offer to pay my fare for a visit. We didn't deliberate for long. After talking to

Tim's sister Jan, I booked flights for the beginning of September: she would come to Hobart to spend some time with Tim while I went to see my rapidly growing granddaughter for a few precious days.

The good timing continued. Brad Hollingsworth called the next morning to update me on the latest hearing, which had been held over two days in the last week of June. He was very happy to hear of my impending visit to the West and I was, in turn, relieved to hear from him, since the *West Australian* newspaper was now, quite understandably, expecting its online readers to subscribe in order to continue to receive in-depth reports. I had in fact decided to do this before the next hearing, feeling that it was important for me to keep up to date with all the details that were emerging as the legal proceedings continued. Brad had confirmed that my access to this public information would in no way compromise my evidence, because Edwards had already been convicted of the crime against me. In the meantime it was good to get another update directly from Brad.

Much of that two-day hearing, Brad told me, had been taken up with legal discussions relating to what the prosecution contended was an emerging pattern of dysfunctional behaviour linked to any emotional turmoil experienced by Edwards over many years. Specific events including relationship break-ups, an affair, a pregnancy, a divorce and a property settlement all correlated in time to the crimes he was alleged to have committed. This information was not surprising to me, given the emphasis placed by the Telecom manager on the 'relationship problems' he'd apparently been having at the time of his attack on me. Carmel Barbagallo revealed that she would be calling several witnesses from Edwards' life over the past thirty years, including partners, friends and workmates. She said that the prosecution's testimony would paint a picture of an emotionally constricted man whose 'inner torment' had emerged in unthinkable brutality. She further stated that prosecution witnesses would reveal that Edwards' fetish for women's underwear had already been evident when he'd been caught, as a thirteen-year-old, rifling through a family friend's underwear drawer. Further witness statements and other evidence would show, she said, that this fixation had escalated until the time of his arrest in 2016, when police had discovered semen-stained female undergarments in his home computer room.

Other witnesses to be called for the prosecution would testify that Edwards was familiar with the Claremont area, having worked on projects including Challenge Stadium (now HBF Stadium), just ten minutes from the centre of Claremont, before the time of the murders. When he was arrested, Edwards had maintained that he had no connection with the Claremont area. Another witness for the prosecution claimed to have seen a Telstra van parked at Karrakatta Cemetery on several occasions in October 1995. This was just after the seventeen-year-old woman was raped, and before the first murder. The prosecution maintained that this behaviour was that of someone sitting in wait for young women to abduct, and that it was related to the behaviour described by other witnesses who recalled a man in a Telstra van approaching women and offering them lifts in 1995 and 1996. I wondered again whether this information had been followed up by the Macro team at the time. The defence team again questioned the relevance of this evidence, maintaining that these incidents demonstrated quite different behaviours.

It was revealed that the prosecution team believed they had DNA evidence that categorically proved that Edwards was the rapist at Karrakatta Cemetery. In an unexpected twist, it was also revealed that the defence team was proposing to show that Edwards had an alibi for Australia Day 1996, the day Sarah Spiers went missing.

Brad talked about the new 'e-trial' technology that was being tested for the first time during this case. Supreme Court staff had developed a system that would allow lawyers and judges to immediately access and view any evidence required. For this trial, more than 1.5 million pages of evidence had been individually numbered, cross-referenced, and uploaded to a massive computer database. These documents, videos and photographs would be able to be flashed up on screens in the courtroom to be viewed by the judge, lawyers, the public gallery and the accused. To prevent unnecessary distress, however, Justice Hall had said that extremely sensitive photos would be viewed in hard copy only by those who needed to see them.

Before we finished our conversation, Brad booked me in for a pre-trial meeting with Carmel Barbagallo on the morning of 4 September, to go over my evidence and prepare for the trial. He also said he would arrange for Katy to pick me up and join us at the meeting.

Later that day, reading over the media reports from the hearing, I was able for the first time to gain a little more insight into what had happened to Edwards after his assault on me. He had reportedly been interviewed by a psychiatrist and a psychologist, whose reports had been presented at his sentencing in the Court of Petty Sessions in June 1990. They described him as 'emotionally constricted', insecure and with fragile self-esteem, a person who experienced intense anger when he felt betrayed or let down in close relationships. The reports suggested that his actions reflected a displacement of feelings and a distortion of perception when he was in a 'highly emotional, aroused state'. There were no more details of the counselling or the sexual offenders' program he'd been ordered to undertake, but the information presented in court was enough to send a shiver down my spine because it showed that he had, indeed, been identified at the time as being emotionally very disturbed. That, together with the completely unprovoked circumstances of his attack on me, had surely warranted some sort of follow-up, and I wondered again what details of this would emerge in the trial.

The next hearing was due to be held in August. As I settled back into our winter hibernation and looked forward to my visit to Perth, I continued to speculate whether any new evidence would be proposed for consideration and whether any of the evidence presented by the prosecution over the previous few days would be challenged by the defence.

11

For the remainder of June and July, with little news from the West, the trial once again took on a faraway and slightly surreal quality. The winter days were short in Hobart, and everyone tried to get home early before the long, cold nights set in. During this time, Tim's application to access the National Disability Insurance Scheme was approved, and we were busy organising support. We were very grateful for this assistance, having coped with his MS by ourselves for more than twenty years. Appointments with GPs, physiotherapists, occupational therapists and exercise physiologists took up much of our time over these months, as well as meetings with support workers who would assist with certain daily activities. With all these added appointments, there was little time left during the day other than to shop, cook, eat and take the dog for walks. Life was very full.

During those long winter evenings before my short trip to Perth to see Kate and her family and meet with Carmel Barbagallo, I spoke with all my family and friends in the West, checked their availability for lunch, dinner, an overnight stay, planning my time away. I talked with Tim's sister who would come to stay with Tim while I was away, explained the new supports, the routine we had settled into. Any spare evening hours were spent piecing together a colourful mosaic I was making for my granddaughter in Perth. Insulated in the depths of a Hobart winter, I could, for just a little while, hardly even imagine the drama that would be associated with my proposed court appearance the following year.

A text from Brad Hollingsworth on the evening of 9 August broke my winter bubble. It came as I was serving up dinner to friends, just five minutes after they had enquired as to the progress of the trial. I had just been thinking that there must be another pre-trial hearing due soon. The text was very apologetic: he wondered whether it was too late to give me a call to update me on that day's hearing, or whether I would prefer to speak over the weekend or on Monday. He told me not to be alarmed at the media reports, saying that they had 'conflated' two issues, portraying the prosecution's situation 'in a worse light than it actually is'.

I looked around the table, poured another glass of wine and replied to his text: 'Monday fine Brad ... have yourself a weekend.' He replied, reiterating that he was available sooner if I wanted to touch base. I was grateful for his contact and support, but at the same time increasingly aware of the infiltration of this lengthy ongoing process in my life.

Brad's text had unsettled me, and when our friends left I reached for my phone to check the latest news from the West. It seemed that Justice Hall had admonished the prosecution team after it had emerged during the day's hearing that a further two-day hearing would be required to deal with potential new evidence. The judge had reminded the prosecutors that earlier in the year he had ordered that no new evidence would be admitted unless it could be deemed significant. He had ruled out several of the prosecution's proposed new items of evidence.

My interest was heightened by a mention of the Hollywood Hospital attack: Justice Hall had reportedly ruled out some 'not presently relevant' evidence from Edwards' first wife relating to what he had told her about the incident at the time. I would, of course, very much have liked to know just what he'd said to her.

I wondered how much Justice Hall's rulings would affect the prosecution's attempt to portray a clear picture of the escalation of an increasingly disturbed and violent offender. Even without the evidence that had now been ruled inadmissible, Edwards' evolving personal history was beginning to demonstrate a high level of emotional instability, clear opportunities, and links to each of the crime scenes.

I was once again drawn in to proceedings in the West, and by the time Brad called on Monday he could tell me nothing new; I had already scoured all the available news. We merely confirmed the arrangements relating to my September appointment with Carmel Barbagallo.

* * *

My flight to Perth was direct from Hobart but long, and extended by strong headwinds. Two seats behind me there was a distressed baby who screamed incessantly, despite all parental and flight attendant attempts to calm him. I was relieved when we landed, and I retrieved my luggage and walked out of the terminal to a loving hug from Sue, Tim's sister.

My granddaughter had changed so much in the eight months since I'd last seen her. She was now nearly three, tall for her age, very vocal and so active it was sometimes hard to keep up with her. As my daughter and I walked together through the quiet leafy streets around her home, she sped ahead on her scooter, pulling abruptly to a halt at each kerbside to check for passing cars. I was amazed at her road sense. We ate breakfast and sometimes lunch at different waterside restaurants, relaxed in the sunshine, read stories and made cups of tea for her teddies and dolls. We shared some special moments together and I was thankful for this time with them.

It was on the Wednesday morning of that week that Katy arrived to pick me up for my meeting with Carmel Barbagallo. It was good to see her again, and we chatted in the car before grabbing a takeaway coffee and heading through security into the DPP building. This time, we were met by an older man whom Katy introduced as a member of the original Macro Task Force. He was friendly and polite, but I was immediately assailed by conflicting thoughts and emotions. I wondered whether he was one of the investigators who had focused so long and so hard on certain potential avenues at the expense of broadening their sights to include other relevant clues and sightings.

We waited in the lobby, and after a few moments Brad came out, accompanied by an assistant. Brad seemed happy to see me, asked about my trip and explained that he would not be in the meeting, but that two other members of the team would be there along with Ms Barbagallo, to go through my evidence with me. He showed me a laptop that had been set up in the lobby, and asked me to watch a twenty-minute video of Ms Barbagallo going through the court process. This was part of my preparation to give evidence, he explained, to familiarise me with the court proceedings. I was offered tea or coffee, shown the basics on the laptop and left to it. On the screen, using simple clear language, Ms Barbagallo explained the court procedure from the time of arrival at the building to the point where the evidence has finished being presented. I wondered how many times this video had been watched, how many more witnesses would yet go through this process before the trial started.

Before I'd had time to process what I had just seen, the assistant came out to tell me that Ms Barbagallo was ready to see me. She ushered me in and introduced me to her – as Carmel – and a colleague called Tara. We shook hands. Carmel was smaller than I had imagined, but intense, with energy radiating out of every pore. I could see that she was already assessing me, gauging what I might say, how I would cope, what questions to ask me, and I felt that the trial was in safe hands. Looking past her, I was once again astounded by that magnificent view over the beautiful Swan River.

After confirming that I had no questions about the video I'd just viewed, Carmel said that she would begin by asking me some questions, 'similar to the trial process', that I would need to answer as clearly and honestly as I could, and that Tara would be taking notes that may be used to add to my statement. Carmel asked whether I was anxious and, although I said no, I realised that, not for the first time, I did feel very intimidated. Perhaps it was the impact of the video – the virtual tour of the courtroom, the emphasis on the solemnity of the proceedings, the formalities of the legal system. So used to the casualness of the Hobart lifestyle, I was suddenly wondering whether I even had suitable 'formal clothing' to wear for my appearance.

With little further preamble, Carmel got straight to the point and asked me to outline what had happened on that day in May 1990 when I was working at Hollywood Hospital. I started telling my story, and could feel myself gaining some confidence but, when I got to the point of being grabbed from behind with something over my mouth, she stopped me abruptly to ask which hand had put the cloth over my mouth. Without hesitation, I said his right hand; the arm had come from my right, had pulled me backwards while his left arm had come around my body, making it almost impossible to move. She asked again if I was sure it was his right hand, and I started to worry that I had got it wrong, but no, I was very sure. Tara passed over a small stack of photographs and asked whether I recognised them. They were of the inside and outside of a small yellow weatherboard annexe-like structure with landscaped surrounds. I felt confused until I saw a photo with three windows looking out, one with a desk underneath and a chair with its back to an alcove with a door leading off it, another of a half-dismantled telephone switchboard system covering a wall, and another of a grubby little toilet room with a badly stained sink. I tried to orient myself.

Carmel passed me copies of the sketches that I had made some two-and-a-half years earlier when Katy and Brendan had come to Hobart to take my statement. Focusing on the attack, looking at the photos, my recollection of the space became confused. Was that the door to the ward? Surely the space between my office chair and the door to the utility room had been bigger? I recognised the outlook from the windows, but it was different in the photos – landscaped now, not grassed. There was no alcove leading to the toilet area; I remembered a curtained glass door that opened directly into a small utility area, a room that could be locked from the inside, a room that led to the toilet, another lockable area. Someone mentioned renovations, and I took a deep breath, slowed my racing mind and I said, 'Yes, that is the office, but it is quite different in these photos.' I felt a little sick and, as if sensing my disquiet, Carmel agreed that it must look quite different now. I was shaken. My memory of the incident was so clear, but what remained of the surroundings in which it had occurred was unfamiliar and confusing. I was thrown by those photos.

Carmel moved back to the attack, and asked about what had been put over my mouth. Was it a tissue? A handkerchief? A cloth? I was unsure: definitely not a tissue; heavier than a handkerchief. I had been sure there was something on it, something to render me unconscious, helpless. I had been terrified. He'd hoiked me up on my chair and pulled me backwards, I had twisted around and the chair had clattered over, I'd fought so hard. I'd kicked him, my shoe had come off. He'd suddenly stopped, I'd fallen back, stared at him, and he was repeating, 'I'm sorry, I'm sorry, I'm sorry'. I thought he might have been crying.

She asked whether I remembered anything about his appearance.

'Tall,' I said. 'My head came to his chest. Big. His arms completely enveloped me. Strong. So strong, I thought I was going to die.'

'Did he have anything distinguishing about his voice? An accent?'

'No.'

'His skin colour?'

'Caucasian, but tanned.'

'His hair?'

'Black. Dark. Thick,' I said, and made movements with my hands to describe the shape.

'What does this mean?' she asked, mirroring my movements.

'Wavy,' I said. 'Parted on the side. And dark, liquid eyes.'

Wanting her to understand how violated I had felt, I added that I had been so traumatised after the incident that I could not bear to remain in that workplace. Because of the attack, I had left the job I loved, the career that I had just been establishing.

Almost inaudibly, Carmel murmured, 'I didn't know that.'

Not yet quite finished, she asked me whether I remembered what I'd been wearing on the day of the incident.

'Not really,' I replied. 'My usual work clothes, I would think: black skirt or trousers and a coloured shirt, probably. Definitely a black cardigan: it was pulled half off in the struggle.'

I told her that I did, however, remember that I'd been wearing my favourite shoes and, as I described them, she pushed an enlarged photograph of those shoes across the table towards me.

'Ah, yes,' she said. 'The Dorothy shoes.' She smiled. 'They would have been my favourites too.'

Carmel's final questions in that meeting related to what had happened after the attack. I told her that, before Edwards had faced court, there had been a meeting with his Telecom manager, that Dave had been present but Edwards had not, that I was not sure where it had been held but I thought it was at a police station near Swanbourne. I told her that the manager had advocated for Edwards, that I had been so angry and upset that nobody had seemed to understand the violence of the attack, that nobody had seemed to be listening to what I was saying.

I wasn't sure how to feel when Carmel said, 'Okay, that's about it.'

I wanted to talk more about the meeting with the Telecom manager. After seeing the photos of the separate little annexe at the back of the palliative care ward, I wanted to ask if she knew why Edwards hadn't been charged with attempted abduction, attempted deprivation of liberty or, given the unprovoked and violent nature of the attack and the clear evidence of bruising to my neck, at least aggravated assault. Why, when he had been ordered to attend a sexual offenders' program, he had only been charged with common assault. But, realising the inappropriateness of such a discussion, and that she was busy and wanting to wind up the meeting so she could turn to other, perhaps more pressing matters, I swallowed my questions. Again reading my stress, Carmel reiterated that I could ask to present my evidence by video link from a separate room if I thought it would be too stressful for me to appear in person. I still had time to think about it.

Before we parted, Carmel asked if I would like to go over to the Supreme Court to familiarise myself with the environment, but by then I was very tired and I had made arrangements to have lunch with Kate. I asked when it would be possible for me to arrange flights for my court appearance, as I had a lot to organise at home. She apologised for all the delays and said she would have much more of an idea of timelines by Christmas. My appearance would probably be in February or even March, she said. After two days in Perth with a taste of the warming weather and the freeway traffic, I was having second thoughts about an extended stay with Tim in the height of summer. I doubted he would cope with the heat.

Leaving the office with Katy, I felt a little overwhelmed, a little confused, a little uncertain, and I wondered once again just what the impending trial would reveal about the past behaviour of Bradley Edwards and about the details of his attack on me at Hollywood Hospital. Katy had obviously been thinking about things as well. As we drove away from the city centre, she reflected on the process of Edwards' arrest and subsequent charging in 1990. She thought that Edwards' father had also been working at Telecom at the time of Edwards' arrest. This was something that, until this point, I had not been aware of. As we talked, I began to wonder just who had organised that meeting in the days following the attack on me, and who the person was that we had met with. During the meeting, Dave and I had both emphasised that the attack had been totally unprovoked, that I had been injured, that I was traumatised, that we felt that Edwards' behaviour had not been normal. I had fully expected Edwards to lose his job, and was bitterly disappointed and terribly angry when he was only charged with common assault. That minor charge had effectively kept Edwards off the police radar for any further serious crimes, and I now wondered what exactly had happened after Dave and I had left the meeting. Why, if he was only charged with common assault, was Edwards ordered to attend a sexual offenders' program? So many questions. Again. Still.

My flight home was shorter than my flight to Perth. What had been a headwind had become a tailwind, there were no screaming infants and I had three seats to myself. A cool crisp Tasmanian breeze met me as I stepped off the plane, and I was glad to be home. Driving from the airport, I thought about my meeting with the DPP team, the hustle and bustle of Perth, the impending hot summer, the total disruption that a month in Perth would cause both Tim and me. My energy was waning. The process of bringing Bradley Edwards to justice had taken up too much of my time already and I was struggling, both with the memories and with what was happening now.

12

It was now a matter of weeks before the trial was due to start. After some discussion with Tim and our family over the days following my trip to Perth, I emailed Brad to say that I would now be coming alone for the trial, and only for the time that was necessary.

And then suddenly, just weeks before the trial was due to start, something happened that changed everything – for the families, for the other living victims, for the prosecution, for the defence and, it would seem, for me.

At a pre-trial hearing on 21 October 2019, Bradley Edwards pleaded guilty to the Huntingdale charges and to the rape in Karrakatta Cemetery in 1996.

The news saturated every media outlet in Western Australia. Edwards had appeared in court, standing impassively as the charges were read out to him, his head falling when Justice Hall spoke of the deliberate degradation and humiliation of his young victim at the cemetery. His guilty pleas were almost inaudible.

Curiously, my first thoughts on hearing the news were about Edwards' family. All their alarm bells must surely now be ringing. There was no question that the Karrakatta rape had been brutal and degrading, the Huntingdale behaviour perverted and threatening. If they had ever held any doubts about his capacity for violent crime, those doubts must surely have been exploded by these confessions, any trust in his innocence now eroded.

The fathers of Sarah Spiers and Ciara Glennon, along with Edwards' two other living victims, had been in court, primed to hear both the confessions and the chain of events that had finally led to Edwards' arrest. At last, the prosecution revealed how everything had come together.

In 1988, the discarded kimono found at the scene of an attack on a young woman in Huntingdale had been placed in an evidence box, where it had lain undisturbed for nearly thirty years. In 2016, cold case detectives, armed with new DNA technology, had found that samples taken from Ciara Glennon's body matched with evidence retained from the 1995 rape of a seventeen-year-old woman in Karrakatta Cemetery. Now understanding that whoever had killed Ciara had been active prior to the killings, detectives had broadened their investigations and, revisiting earlier crimes, re-examined the kimono. They found that it was stained with traceable DNA samples that matched those taken from Ciara and from the Karrakatta victim. Connecting the Huntingdale kimono assault to several unusual break-ins in the same area in 1998, during which women's underwear and nightclothes had been stolen from clotheslines and houses, they realised that fingerprint evidence taken from those crimes might also be significant. When those fingerprints were run through the national database, they matched with a record of their owner: Bradley Robert Edwards, identified and fingerprinted in 1990 when he'd been charged with assaulting me at Hollywood Hospital.

Police had then begun a covert surveillance operation, watching the seemingly ordinary and inoffensive Telstra worker going about his business. During their surveillance, an operator managed to retrieve a discarded soft-drink bottle on which Edwards had left his DNA. When this remnant was tested, it matched the samples taken from Ciara and the Karrakatta rape victim, and Edwards was arrested. Formal DNA samples taken from him at the time of his arrest confirmed the matches.

It all sounded so clear, so simple, so obvious, all the dots finally joining up, order out of chaos, answers now emerging where before there were only questions.

During the hearing, the prosecution had revealed a report by a British profiler, which stated that DNA from Edwards found under Ciara's fingernails was either from passive contact or from her scratching him, but definitely through contact. Other significant news related to the fibre evidence. Tiny blue polyester fibres found on the clothing of the Karrakatta rape victim had been found to be the same type of fibres found on the bodies of Ciara Glennon and Jane Rimmer, and in the Holden Commodore Telstra work car driven by Edwards at the time the crimes were committed. These fibres were common to the work trousers issued to Telstra workers at the time.

Carmel Barbagallo had reiterated the prosecution's wish to include their theory of motivation, correlating 'spikes' in Edwards' emotional state relating to his reaction to relationship issues with the timeline of the crimes. I could feel this theory resonating strongly with my own experience. Recalling the Telecom manager's reference to Edwards' stressful 'relationship problems', I also remembered my response: that this was not a normal reaction. People do not randomly and violently attack other people just because they are having relationship problems.

On the evening of the hearing, I received a text from Katy asking whether I had heard the good news. She sounded almost jubilant. Confessions are usually hard won; these were a huge bonus to the case. They meant that Edwards' other living victims would not have to face him in court, would not have to relive every excruciating moment of their terrible experiences. They must have been so relieved to hear this news.

I wondered what this latest development meant for me. Now that Edwards' past deviant and obviously increasingly violent behaviour was officially on record, perhaps there would be no need for me to tell my story. I realised I was not sure how I felt about this. The impending trial and my probable court appearance had overshadowed my life for the past three years. There had been ongoing contact with the police and the DPP, extensive media coverage and great interest from family and friends, all of which had caused me to continually relive some of the trauma of the attack and its aftermath. The writing down of my experiences, while cathartic, had at times also exacerbated that trauma. The continual playing out of emotions that had previously been long buried had not been easy.

As I thought more about the day's developments, I experienced many conflicting emotions. What had happened to me all those years ago had been, I believed, effectively played down by the police and by Telecom, almost certainly resulting in Edwards receiving a lesser sentence than the crime warranted. My experience had been invalidated. I had been told that there was not enough evidence to charge him with anything more serious than common assault. At the time, I did not understand why that was the case, and I still did not. Although brief, it was a violent attack, and there had clearly been some degree of premeditation. I believe he had surveyed the ward and ensured that the coast was clear before he came back and stood behind me. He had attempted to muffle my cries for help with a cloth. He had cable ties in his pocket, and he had tried to drag me to a secluded spot. I had sustained bruising and been totally traumatised. And I now understood that he had been ordered to attend a sexual offenders' program as a result of the incident. The experience had caused me to leave my job, my career, had affected my confidence, my relationships, my trust in people and the systems around me that were supposed to protect me. Why had nobody understood all this? Why had nobody listened?

A phone call from Brad Hollingsworth interrupted my jumbled thoughts. He sounded busy, happy. I told him that Tim and I had been following the news. Confirming my thoughts, he suggested that, considering Edwards' confessions, Justice Hall might very well now feel the trial should be based mainly on forensic evidence. There would perhaps be no need to show his motivation, the links with periods of emotional turmoil, the development of a killer. These things were in any case difficult to prove, very complex, open to other interpretations, always arguable. Brad mentioned that the professionals who had written the pre-trial psychological reports at the time of Edwards' sentencing in 1990 now had no recollection of him at all. I was not surprised. For thirty years he had been blending in to his local community, even while he was allegedly committing murders.

Brad said he didn't know what the judge's ruling would be, but that the costs associated with the trial, the number of witnesses, the length of time in court, would all be reduced and that surely was a good thing. In light of the confessions, the prosecution would now need to work hard to restructure its case, taking into consideration the reduced time frame. There might well be another delay in the start date, but hopefully that would be minor. There were other matters for Justice Hall to deal with, other rulings to come. Brad said he would be in touch as things became clearer.

The call from Brad grounded me a little, gave me a bit of perspective on what had just transpired. Like everyone mesmerised by this ongoing prosecution, I wondered why, at this stage in the proceedings, Edwards had confessed. Leading WA Queen's Counsel Tom Percy expressed some thoughts on this in the following day's *West Australian*. He suggested that the guilty pleas might represent a change of heart for the accused, or they could be a tactical ploy by the defence. The tactical advantages of a guilty plea included the removal of 'indefensible' offences to focus on what could be perceived as 'more defensible' charges, and the portrayal of the defendant as honest, admitting to charges he was guilty of, denying those he did not commit. With respect to the admissibility of the guilty pleas as evidence in the murder trial, Mr Percy said that would depend on the prosecution's presentation of a case for propensity for violent assault, something the defence was likely to strongly contest. Considering sentencing, the guilty pleas would attract six to eight years imprisonment plus ongoing indefinite detention, subject to dangerous sex offender legislation. If he was found guilty of murder, Edwards would receive a life sentence and, according to Western Australian law, no other sentence could be cumulative on a life sentence.

* * *

Over the next week, Brad and I played phone tag. When we finally talked there was a definite change in his tone. He was apologetic for not getting hold of me earlier, and his voice was gentle, his words less hurried than they had been in the past.

Stressing that he still could not say anything definitive, he was clearer about my future role in the trial. It was now likely to be that of an observer. He felt that, now they had Edwards' confessions relating to the other two living victims, Justice Hall would rule out the necessity for those women to appear as witnesses. Instead, statements relating to the attacks would likely be read out in court at a relevant time as the prosecution was building up its case. Brad asked how I felt about this, particularly given that my story had not been heard all those years ago.

Before I answered, and seemingly thinking aloud, he suggested that I might fly over anyway, to be present in court with the other women when our stories were read out. It was obvious that he understood that, for me, this trial was an opportunity to finally be heard, for everyone to finally understand that Edwards' attack on me had not just been an isolated 'incident' that had warranted a somewhat meagre punishment, but one in a series of escalatingly violent attacks that had ultimately resulted in unimaginable outcomes for so many people.

I told him I had very mixed feelings. Yes, after three years of ongoing contact with the WA police and the DPP, a part of me felt robbed, in some sense dismissed and almost negated again with these latest developments. But an even bigger part of me was so relieved that I would not have to go through the ordeal of appearing in the WA Supreme Court, the stress of facing Edwards, another round of long flights and being away from home.

I thought then that this might well be my last contact with Brad and the DPP. They had my statement, they had everything they needed from me to complete my part in this terrible story. It was clear to me that Brad and his team had all acknowledged my past ordeal, and perhaps that was enough. They now needed to focus on shoring up all the evidence they needed to present to convict a killer.

My final thoughts after what seemed like a long week were about confessions. Rereading the damning headlines from the *West Australian*, I thought back to Edwards' Telecom manager's comments about his employee's 'sensitivity', and I wondered just how Edwards was dealing with the media's open loathing, if he was in fact aware of the press reports. I wondered whether his admissions of evil brutality would cause his family, his supporters to look at him differently, and whether those looks would cause him to break down, to confess to the murders, to finally let Sarah Spiers' family know just where her remains could be found.

So sure that something must have shifted for Edwards, so wanting to effect this outcome, I sent a text to Katy: 'Just so it's on record, I reckon he's going to confess to the murders.' Her response was immediate: 'I really hope you're right.'

13

As we moved into November, the weather started to warm up and we had visitors from the mainland. Old friends, old colleagues, good food, fine wine, lots of reminiscing. We were settling well into our new routine at home with the additional support for Tim. A community agency now sent Will twice a week to help Tim with strength-building exercises, which he'd become increasingly unable to do on his own as his mobility and balance deteriorated. A big, kindly man, Will had temporarily left his life in Western Australia to come to Hobart to care for his ninety-four-year-old mother. He told us she was strong and healthy for her age, and I hoped that both she and he would be with us for a long time. He and Tim went to the physio together, developed an exercise plan, and I sometimes listened to them chatting happily as he guided Tim through the routine. There was lots of laughter; it was like having a very friendly, caring personal trainer. A massage therapist also visited monthly to help Tim with the stiffness and cramps, and a mobile podiatrist and a neighbour who is a hairdresser were also happy to come to the house as needed. All this assistance had taken away some of the responsibility I had previously felt for helping Tim to maintain his health, and I was pleased and grateful.

As the trial loomed closer, my thoughts often drifted to the prosecution team. I imagined them to be frantically busy, contacting witnesses, shoring up statements, arranging and rearranging scheduled appearances, maximising the proposed impact of the evidence against Edwards, attempting to minimise the defence's arguments.

The media had been releasing little snippets of information relating to continued rulings from Justice Hall about allowable evidence, which was apparently still trickling in. I read somewhere that the security guard from Hollywood Hospital would be called as a witness, but a witness to what? He hadn't seen the attack; nobody had. He'd seen a dazed, seemingly repentant man standing alone in a room, waiting for police to arrive. What would he be able to say to help the prosecution's case? The police who'd attended after the attack might also be called. Would they remember anything after all these years? And if any of them was being called up, surely I would be too? I wondered whether the Telecom manager we'd met with after the attack had provided a witness statement. Did he remember how strongly he'd advocated for his subordinate? Had he conferred with the police regarding the charge after Dave and I had left the building? So many thoughts and questions swam around in my mind.

My friend Sheila called and, after a long chat catching up on all our respective family news, she mentioned that Channel 7 would be airing a segment about the Claremont killings that night. Tim and I watched the report. It drew together the basic story leading to the arrest of Edwards, presenting it as a simple chronological series of events. As I listened to veteran WA reporter Alison Fan briefly mention the Hollywood Hospital attack, I wondered whether she was questioning why Edwards wasn't charged with something more serious at the time. At the end of the segment, I watched Jane Rimmer's brother, obviously emotional and still grieving more than twenty years after her terrible murder, and I thought then that perhaps the families of those young women who were so tragically and brutally taken from them wouldn't want to hear that Edwards might have been stopped long ago. Perhaps it was enough for them to catch the person responsible, to punish him.

By mid-November, there was no escape from the build-up to the start of the trial. Justice Hall had released further rulings on the admissibility of evidence, and that information had kickstarted the Western Australian media into more intense action, with reports in the weekend papers and another segment on Channel 7 that was then highlighted in the *West Australian*.

One of the rulings related to the admissibility of evidence regarding motive. Justice Hall had indicated that the prosecution would be allowed to present its theory that, beginning with the Hollywood Hospital attack and escalating to the Claremont murders, upsets in Edwards' emotional state had led to the committal of violent crimes against unknown and unsuspecting women. Edwards himself had indicated, in the psychologist's report prepared after he'd pleaded guilty to his attack on me, that he'd been 'deeply distressed' by his wife's recent infidelity. It seemed, though, that he'd been unable to explain exactly why he'd attacked me. Justice Hall had accepted the relationship between emotional stress and the attack on me, but was not convinced that such a clear relationship could be established between Edwards' emotional state and the murders.

I was of course continually wondering what, if any, impact these latest rulings would have on me. Would the presentation of the police report and the psychological report relating to Edwards' attack on me be enough to demonstrate the connection to his emotional state, or would the judge decide that it would be important to hear my evidence as well?

One evening, as I was thinking all this through, I received an unexpected text from Brad Hollingsworth. He apologised for not contacting me sooner, and said that the situation with my evidence was still unresolved but should become clearer in the next week or so, and that he would phone me about it at some stage. He also directed me to the WA government's online Courts Portal, which detailed the latest decisions by Justice Hall.

Although it added to my understanding of the emotional upset ruling, the information on the portal made for some very intense and jargonistic reading, and some of the details I found quite distressing. These included quotes from the psychologist's report describing Edwards' account of his attack on me: 'He asked for directions to the nearest toilet ...' *He didn't. He asked if he could use the toilet, which indicated to me that he knew where the toilet was.* 'He was directed down the hall ...' *He wasn't. The toilet was off the room behind me.* 'He used the toilet and went back to work ...' *He didn't. He wasn't in there long enough to use the toilet. And I don't think he went back to work, I think he went to the ward door to check that no-one was around.* 'He placed a dishcloth over her mouth and grabbed her around the waist, she struggled and screamed ... he then realised what was happening, let her go and apologised ...' *He didn't. He grabbed me from behind, around my neck and shoulders, effectively pinning my arms to my sides, and pushed a cloth into my mouth as he pulled me backwards and upwards on my chair. I was unable to make a sound. When I realised there was nothing on the cloth to render me unconscious, I struggled for my life, managed to twist around, the chair clattered over and I kicked him. It was then that he stopped abruptly, saying over and over, 'I'm sorry, I'm sorry, I'm sorry'.*

The judge also repeated an earlier summary of the Hollywood Hospital incident as propensity evidence, stating at the end: 'A hospital security guard attended and detained the accused until police arrived. The accused admitted to the security guard that he had tried to drag the complainant to the toilet cubicle. He was found to have cable ties in his pocket, though such ties could be used in the course of his work'. This was the first I had heard of Edwards' admission that he had, in fact, been trying to abduct me. *I'd* known this, of course, and so had the security guard, it now seemed. So why had that not counted as attempted abduction? Reading the findings, I could feel my anger, my fury, rising.

The other part of the rulings that caused me some consternation was in Justice Hall's summation. He commented that: 'The differences between the Hollywood Hospital incident and [the murders] need to be taken into account. They include, that the Hollywood Hospital incident occurred in the daytime, in a workplace, did not involve abduction and that the accused stopped voluntarily, without harming the victim ... it would seem to have been an opportunistic attack, consistent with it arising from an irrational response to personal trauma'. *No abduction? No harm? Stopped voluntarily? Opportunistic?*

After some consideration, I decided to send a message to Brad. I wanted to express my feelings about the rulings, something he might perhaps have been anticipating when he'd sent the link to the portal. I told him that, given that I now knew that Edwards had admitted at the time to trying to drag me into the toilet, I was somewhat confused and extremely angry that he was not then charged with at least attempted abduction. I also expressed my disappointment at the judge's lack of recognition of the injuries I had sustained in the attack. Although I am of course extremely thankful that I was not raped or, even worse,

Edwards did not carry out his attack on me 'without harming the victim'. I was bruised and traumatised. It was violent.

Brad called me almost immediately. Acknowledging the points I had made, he asked whether there had been any mention of injuries in my witness statement. I told him yes, that, fearing possible whiplash and mindful of a possible worker's compensation claim, I'd seen a doctor, and that Katy had said she would try to follow this up with Medicare but that it was such a long time ago the records might be hard to come by. I also told him that I did not believe that Edwards had voluntarily stopped the attack: he'd stopped because I'd struggled, because I'd kicked him hard, because the chair had clattered over, because the cloth had fallen on the floor and he'd realised I would be able to scream – all things that he had not been expecting to happen when he'd begun to attack me.

Brad listened intently to everything I had to say. He then said that everyone involved in the prosecution's case understood the trauma and the violence of Edwards' attack on me, and that they were all wondering too why he was not charged with a more serious offence at the time, one that might have brought him to the attention of the police investigating the Claremont killings in the mid-1990s, perhaps even halting his alleged violent rampage.

I found his comment to be at the same time validating and deeply, tragically disturbing.

Catharsis

1

What would turn out to be one of the longest-running and most expensive murder trials in Australia's history finally began before the Supreme Court of Western Australia on Monday 25 November 2019. Held in a courtroom on the seventh floor of the District Court building on Hay Street, the trial was simultaneously screened on monitors in the Supreme Court building on Barrack Street, with both venues offering limited but open seating in the public gallery.

My prediction that Bradley Edwards might confess beforehand to the Claremont killings had obviously been proven wrong. In fact, I could now see that his thinking had not changed since 1990. At that time, perhaps responding to legal advice provided to him with the intention of reducing the likelihood of a prison sentence, he'd pleaded guilty to the lesser charge of common assault. It had worked for him then: he had remained free, sentenced only to probation and an order to attend a sexual offenders' program. He had kept his job. Now it seemed he was taking a similar approach: plead guilty to the 'lesser' offences and he might be let off the murder charges. At least I was quite sure that this time around, whatever the outcome of the trial, his life would never be the same.

Before the trial got underway, I sent a text to Brad Hollingsworth wishing him and the rest of the prosecution team well for this last part of what had been, for everyone involved, a terribly long and difficult journey. Tim and I then settled down to follow the live media reports that would closely cover the courtroom events as they unfolded, from the quiet seclusion of our Hobart home.

The media described the victims' families as they arrived at the courthouse: mothers, fathers, brothers and sisters, supporting each other through this, the beginning of the final long ordeal in their heartbreaking journey of the past twenty-five years. As I watched and listened, I wanted to be there, to sit with them as they had to listen to the graphic and horrific details about the fate of their loved ones, details that were now being made public. I wanted to absorb some of their pain and their sorrow for them. I felt so guilty that I had escaped, that I hadn't been listened to, that I hadn't made more of a fuss, that he hadn't been charged with a more serious offence, that I had been able to bury my own trauma, been able to continue living my life.

The *West Australian* that morning had published a comprehensive twelve-page guide to what it referred to as the 'Trial of the Century'. The front-page headlines trumpeted that this was the 'Time for Answers' about what exactly had happened during one of the 'darkest chapters in our history'. The articles laid out the prosecution's case, which would aim to demonstrate how a 'socially awkward teenager' had allegedly developed into a violent rapist and murderer living an otherwise quiet and unremarkable life in suburban Perth. There were overviews of the careers of both Carmel Barbagallo for the prosecution and Paul Yovich for the defence. Clearly, they were both highly experienced senior lawyers, both forces to be reckoned with, and I felt sure that their work over the period of the trial would be long and hard.

Presiding over the proceedings, and solely responsible for the ultimate verdict in this judge-alone trial, Justice Stephen Hall was reported to be particularly experienced in complex cases, and very highly regarded within the Perth legal fraternity. His job in this case was momentous.

As Tim and I sat at home watching the live video feed from the courtroom, Edwards was arraigned on each of the three murder charges, pleading not guilty three times. Justice Hall reminded everyone that the accused was innocent until proven otherwise beyond all reasonable doubt.

Carmel Barbagallo then began outlining the case the prosecution would be presenting in detail to the court over the coming months, bringing together the complete picture, of which only individual disjointed details had been reported as they had been revealed over the previous three years. As she detailed the circumstances of the horrifying Karrakatta rape, the disappearances of the three young women from Claremont, the terrible discovery of the bodies of the two murdered women, I could almost feel the tears being shed in the public gallery. Leaving the court in no doubt as to the prosecution's position, she stated emphatically: 'There was one killer, and that killer is Bradley Robert Edwards.'

The court was spellbound as CCTV footage was shown of Jane Rimmer and of Ciara Glennon outside Claremont's Continental Hotel on the nights they each went missing, and a recording played of Sarah Spiers' phone call to Swan Taxis to book a lift home just before she vanished. Sarah's parents, Don and Carol Spiers; Ciara's father and sister, Denis and Denise Glennon; and Jane's mother, Jenny Rimmer, were all present in the courtroom on that first day. I imagined them all sitting close to each other, sharing whatever strength they were able to muster between them amid their collective heartbreak. Edwards' other living victims, of the Huntingdale and Karrakatta attacks, were also present, able to attend his trial for murder now that he had confessed to his attacks on them.

The media reported that Edwards' face during most of that day's proceedings remained expressionless, his gaze fixed, his eyes closed for long periods.

The second day was much the same as the first. Carmel Barbagallo continued outlining the prosecution's case, detailing the measures that had led to the arrest of Edwards, the DNA and fibre evidence that would be presented and the witnesses that would be called – people involved in various ways in Edwards' life over the previous three decades, people whom she maintained would implicate him in the crimes of which he had been accused.

When she had finished, defence lawyer Paul Yovich took just twenty-five minutes to outline his approach. Focusing on the repudiation of DNA evidence, he was not required to prove Edwards' innocence, but he intended to show that it could not be proved *beyond reasonable doubt* that his client was the killer.

On day two of the trial, we had just finished dinner and I was clearing away the dishes, preparing for an early night, when my mobile rang and I saw that it was Brad Hollingsworth. I thought that he probably just wanted to update me on the proceedings so far. Although grateful for the contact, I was also tired, and felt that I was pretty much up to date already from the live media reporting, so for a moment I considered not answering and calling him back the next day. But I took the call.

He sounded tired but upbeat, and I thought that things must have been proceeding well from the prosecution team's perspective. After a bit of an update, he moved on to the subject of witnesses, saying that they would be calling on Edwards' first wife soon. He then said that they would now definitely be calling me, and that this would be earlier than they had anticipated – 'Probably next Tuesday,' he said.

My adrenaline shot up, and my eyes darted to the wall calendar that pretty much ruled my life. I could see the following week at a glance – Tim's physio appointment, a dentist visit, houseguests arriving from the mainland – and I mumbled something about checking it out and getting back to him in the morning. He then said that they could, at a pinch, make it Thursday, so I quickly replied, 'No, Tuesday's fine. There are direct flights from Hobart on Monday, Wednesday and Friday.' Brad confirmed that DPP staff would liaise with me and organise everything. He also reiterated that I could still elect to give my evidence from a separate room at the courthouse by video link if being in the courtroom would prove too distressing for me.

I spent much of the next morning rescheduling appointments, organising transport for Tim's physio visit, arranging for a friend to walk Maisie while I was away. I called Kate in Perth, who offered to come with me to court. After speaking with Tim, his sister Sue called from Perth to say that she would like to be there to support me as well. Thinking that the public gallery might well be full given the high-profile nature of the case, I messaged DPP staff, who said they would set aside seats for them both. In need of a haircut, I then brought my pre-Christmas hair appointment forward and, finally relaxing as I was being shampooed, I thought that I had made just about all the preparations I could for the following week's journey back across Australia. My hairdresser, Greg, knew of the trial, and I told him that I would now be giving evidence. Sensing my anxiety, he finished blow-drying my hair, gently squeezed my shoulder and, trying to lift my mood, joked: 'Don't worry, no-one will be listening to your evidence – they'll all be wondering who your hairdresser is!' His kindness made me smile, and relax just a little.

I had just one more thing to do. I messaged Katy and asked if she would be there on the day I gave evidence. She responded immediately, expressing some surprise that it would be so soon, but said not to worry, that she would do the necessary liaison and meet me in the lobby of my hotel an hour before I was due in court.

* * *

It was just eleven degrees in Hobart, spitting rain and blowing a gale the day I got into a taxi and headed for the airport. I was to give my evidence the following day – Tuesday 3 December 2019 – and fly home the day after that. Most of my carry-on luggage was made up of Christmas presents for my granddaughter, and I couldn't wait to see her little face again. I wandered around the small airport lounge and headed for the bookstands, trying to normalise the trip in an effort to quell the anxious fluttering that was going on somewhere between my heart and my stomach. It was part of my airport routine to purchase a book to read on the plane, and Hobart Airport usually has a good selection. But as I browsed the titles, my mind was elsewhere: partly in the past, going over all that had happened, and partly in the future, wondering what the following day would bring. I scanned the back cover of a book that caught my eye and, thinking it looked like a good read, bought it. As I settled into my seat after take-off, I opened it and started to read. A few paragraphs in, I realised that it was the same book I'd purchased on my previous trip to Perth – and grimaced, wondering how many times I was going to have to cover the same ground until it was finally over.

2

The hotel in Perth was just a stone's throw from District Court. It was very quiet and comfortable, but my sleep was broken, filled with disturbing dreams of driverless buses hurtling down steep, narrow mountain roads with me, the only passenger, unable to halt the impending crash. I woke early with that wired feeling that you get when your body is running on adrenaline, and I hoped that I would last the day.

At seven am I pressed the buttons that opened the curtains and the blind. Light streamed in through the floor-to-ceiling window, glaring and hot even through the double glazing, and I remembered that the temperature was tipped to reach forty degrees in Perth that day.

I felt slightly sick as I ate the breakfast I'd ordered the night before: a fancy little poached egg that was served beautifully with sparkling cutlery and crisp white linen. Kate and Sue met in the lobby, and I went down in the lift to bring them up to my room for a coffee. They were impressed with the view, but I didn't share their enthusiasm; I was preoccupied with what was to come.

At ten am, Katy called – right on time, an hour before my scheduled appearance. I was waiting. I gathered up my things – my bag, a copy of my evidence – and I looked around the room, knowing that it would seem very different that afternoon when it was all over.

When I walked into the lobby restaurant, Katy was on her phone, looking out of a window. As she swung around and saw me, her face broke into a smile and she stepped forward and gave me a big hug. We chatted and drank more much-needed coffee, and she revealed that her parents were currently in Perth on holiday – that she, in fact, was on holiday, but had come in to work twice to be with witnesses, once the previous week and now again for me. I was grateful. She talked about everything except my impending evidence and, although I still felt anxious, I found myself distracted a little. It was not quite two friends having a catch-up, but close to it.

Katy asked whether I would mind having my photograph taken – a headless photo for the media, she explained, so that they would know what I was wearing, so that they could avoid filming or photographing me because of the suppression order. With this request, the situation took on a slightly surreal feeling, and when she showed me the resulting photograph I started laughing, but then felt guilty because clearly laughter didn't seem appropriate at that time.

As it got closer to eleven am, Katy kept checking her mobile, but in the end, it was me who received a message from a DPP staffer, asking me to let her know when I was arriving so she could come out and greet me. Katy quickly made contact with the DPP team herself, and together we stepped out into the stifling Perth heat.

As we approached the court building, I could see a number of reporters and cameras outside the front of the building. I was relieved when Katy ushered me to a side entrance. We walked through the cafeteria into the lobby, which was dominated by a security screening checkpoint similar to those found at airports. We dropped our bags into the plastic trays provided and stepped through the scanner, then walked over to the lifts and took one up to the seventh floor.

Kate and Sue were waiting for me outside the courtroom. I think I acknowledged them as Katy and I walked past, but I was very focused on where I was heading. The DPP staffer was also waiting for us, and she ushered us into a small room to the side of the courtroom entrance. Here I was introduced to two detectives from the Macro team, but I failed to register their names. I was already overwhelmed.

Against the wall on two sides of the room were chest-high bookshelves containing ringbinder files, all labelled *The State of Western Australia v Bradley Robert Edwards*. There were literally dozens and dozens of these files; I stopped counting at 130. There was a long table and very little room for the half-a-dozen chairs that surrounded it. The three detectives and the paralegal were friendly and comfortable with each other; they had obviously been working together for a while. They offered me water, mints, chocolate. Like Katy had done back at the hotel, they kept chatting to me, keeping things as normal as possible. They also checked in now and again, asking how I was doing. I wished it would all hurry up. I just wanted it to be over.

Just before midday someone came in and, after a hurried conversation with the detectives, informed me that they were no longer sure that my evidence would be required that morning – I might not be called until the afternoon. We waited another hour to be sure.

Someone dropped in a big bundle of papers for me to look at. It was my evidence, plus lots of photographs of the social work office area at Hollywood Hospital, some of which I had previously seen and some that were new to me. The photos helped to bring me back to the reason I was there, and I could feel myself moving back in time as I looked at them, identifying certain details that hadn't changed and making sense of some of the obvious structural changes.

I was asked when had been the last time I'd looked at my evidence, and I replied that it was last Friday. But I knew I didn't need to look at it. It had happened to me. I remembered it.

Suddenly the door opened, and the room was filled with black legal gowns and animated chatter. The trial had adjourned for lunch. Carmel asked me how I was doing, and said it was unlikely now that they would call me before three pm. She suggested that in the meantime I might want to go and get some lunch, and perhaps even have a little nap back at my hotel.

Katy and I made our way out of the room, and I looked to see whether Kate and Sue were around, but they had obviously already left for lunch. I called Kate, who told me they were in a particular restaurant across the road and had just ordered. I said I would join them.

Katy ushered me towards the lifts, across the little foyer that was by now filled with men in suits, one smiling broadly at me in recognition. He looked vaguely familiar, but my brain was not properly in gear in those unfamiliar surroundings. He put out his hand and said warmly, 'Aaron. I came and served you the summons.' I smiled back, wondering whether he had ended up finding somewhere good to eat in Hobart.

Katy stayed close as we exited the lift and made our way back through the cafeteria and out the side door, again avoiding the media. I told her that I would make my own way back to the hotel after lunch for a rest, and she said she would pick me up again just before three pm.

In the restaurant, I ordered pasta but I was not hungry. Kate and Sue made small talk, but I was starting to flag and we didn't hang around long. I made my way back to the hotel, Sue headed back to the court building and Kate wandered off for a bit of retail therapy.

My room was blissfully cool and quiet, and I was just dozing off when Katy rang, urgency in her voice: 'You're needed now.' A quick tidy-up and, grabbing my bag, I headed back down in the lift to the lobby where Katy was waiting, then back out into the blinding heat again. It was the hottest part of the day and the streets were deserted. Even the reporters had gone somewhere cooler, so this time we made for the front entrance, through security and back up to the seventh floor.

As I settled myself back in the little anteroom, I hoped there would not be too much more waiting, as my energy was rapidly fading. In what seemed like no time at all the door opened and a voice said, 'Calling Ms Wendy Davis.' I scrambled to my feet as the attendant called again, this time louder and underscored with a little irritation, which flustered me.

I followed the attendant into the courtroom, which was silent. She nodded respectfully at Justice Hall and I followed her lead, and then we walked at a fast pace past the public gallery. Kate and Sue were both sitting there in the front row, but my gaze was drawn to the tortured figure at the end of the bench. For a brief moment, I locked eyes with Denis Glennon. Almost imperceptibly, he nodded, and I moved on, determined to do my best.

As I stepped into the witness box, I was relieved to see that there was a chair; I felt a little unsteady on my feet. It was a swivelling office chair on wheels and, as I sat down, I glanced over at Bradley Robert Edwards, sitting just a few metres away, once again in the same room as me. The memory of that day twenty-nine years ago came flooding back and, for just a moment, I felt a surge of pure terror. But this time I was ready, and everybody was finally listening.

As I stated my full name, Carmel stood and turned in my direction, solid and reassuring. She asked me to describe my former workplace, my position, my office and its proximity to the ward. The drawings that I had done for Katy and Brendan nearly three years earlier when they had come to Hobart to take my statement now flashed on a screen in front of me, and on a screen on the wall of the courtroom behind Edwards.

Carmel then got straight to the point, asking me to describe what had happened that afternoon. Talking directly to her, I began recounting – and reliving – 'the incident'. At one stage, out of the corner of my eye, I saw Mr Yovich stand and heard him start to interject, but Justice Hall motioned for him to sit down.

The report that was later written up by journalist John Flint and published in the following day's *West Australian* best sums up what I told the courtroom:

> With Bradley Edwards sitting 10m across from her, the diminutive woman in the witness box used her hands and arms to demonstrate how she was attacked from behind during a 10-second struggle with the accused.
>
> It happened 29 years ago but she vividly recalled every horrific second of the attack. 'I honestly thought I was going to die,' the 69-year-old told the court yesterday.
>
> She did not only retell what happened. She re-enacted it as well. She placed a hand over her mouth as she explained Mr Edwards' first move was to place a cloth over her mouth.
>
> Just before the May 1990 assault, she had been sitting at her desk at Hollywood Hospital writing a report she was eager to finish so she could get home early to celebrate her daughter's birthday. It was the quietest part of the day in that part of the hospital. Her office was just off the palliative care ward. The social worker said she knew Telstra technicians were nearby upgrading the phone system.
>
> When the 21-year-old technician asked to use the toilet behind her, she had no reason to feel anything was amiss. She heard the flush. He reappeared then asked for permission to retrieve a pen or pencil he said he had left

> in the cubicle. Just as she was thinking it was odd, a hand came around her face. She was in a fight for her life.
>
> Using her arms to demonstrate how she was 'hoiked up' out of her seat, she twisted and motioned a kick to show prosecutor Carmel Barbagallo how she fought back.
>
> She had stopped breathing because she feared the cloth might have been soaked in chemicals but then realised she had to breathe if she was going to break his tight arm grip under her neck. Those breaths saved her, giving her the strength to keep her feet on the ground. She said she was staggering backwards. He was dragging her towards the toilet.
>
> 'Sorry, it's distressing to relive this,' she said at one point.
>
> Mr Edwards appeared sheepish. He had been taking notes and leaning his face on a hand just prior. Now he was looking down. He pleaded guilty to the attack at the time.
>
> The witness, whose identity cannot be revealed, said she was able to twist around, knocking her chair over and losing a shoe in the melee.
>
> As quickly as the assault started, it stopped. 'I fell back and looked at him,' she said. 'He was saying, "I'm sorry, I'm sorry, I'm sorry". It was the strangest ...'
>
> She did not need to complete the sentence. Everyone understood.

I was surprised when I heard Justice Hall thanking and dismissing me. I had more to say. I wanted to tell them all how there had been a meeting with someone from Telecom management, someone who hadn't listened to me, someone who had advocated strongly for Edwards, someone who had not seemed to understand how strange and violent the attack had been. That the police hadn't interviewed me. That I had been very angry and upset when Edwards was only charged with common assault. But I was dismissed.

I stepped uncertainly out of the witness box and walked back up the aisle towards the public gallery. Glancing at Kate and Sue, I was relieved to see them gathering their things. I needed a hug.

I noticed Ciara Glennon's sister seated next to her father, her face unreadable. As my gaze moved to Denis, he again nodded, ever so slightly, and I was grateful for the acknowledgement. At the same time, I wondered, 'Does he know there is more to my story?'

The day was not yet over. Despite my fatigue and the oppressive heat, I wanted to see my granddaughter, so Kate and I made our way to the carpark and drove the short distance to her home. The toddler was happy, excited to see me, full of life, and the short visit grounded me.

As the last of the adrenaline deserted me, I asked Kate to take me back to the hotel. I was so hungry, and I needed to sleep. After touching base with Tim, I stood under the shower for what seemed like hours, just letting the water wash away everything from the day. Then I opened the small bottle of shiraz in the minibar and ordered a big steak. I was asleep by nine pm.

3

Because my flight home was not until midday the following day, I checked out of the hotel early that morning and made my way back to Kate's for a little more daughter and granddaughter time. My arrival was again greeted with hugs, and with excited demands from the little one who wanted me to play snap, to look at her toy cars, play with her tea set. Their two cats wound around our legs as we made tea to drink while we caught up on family news. I soaked up some cherished time with them before we headed together to the airport and, as I picked up my boarding pass and we all moved through airport security, life felt almost normal again.

That feeling lasted only until we saw the day's newsstands. The headlines jumped out: 'A hand around my face. It had a CLOTH on it ... I thought I was GOING TO DIE'. My account of the attack was on the front page of the *West Australian*, and there was another full spread with more details on pages four and five.

It felt strangely gratifying to me that the details of Edwards' attack on me all those years ago were now there for all to see, but at the same time it didn't feel quite right. It felt unfinished. It was me, but I felt it wasn't. I was unnamed, invisible, my story only half told. I realised I still felt unheard. I looked around at everyone just going about their business, and everything was once again tinged with a sense of unreality. A shout from my granddaughter brought me back to reality, and we hugged for a long time as we said our goodbyes.

The flight was uneventful. I felt so much lighter now that my part in the trial was over. It was evening by the time I stepped off the plane and took some big, deep, grateful breaths of the fresh, cold, clean air of Tasmania. First to the taxi rank, I was keen to get home to the warm welcome I knew would be waiting for me.

As I opened the front door, Maisie nearly knocked me off my feet, almost wagging her tail off and actually smiling at me in that way that only a staffy can. Tim's welcome was less boisterous but equally enthusiastic, and I was so glad to be home.

In the days that followed, my experience of giving evidence and my feeling of unfinished business stayed with me, dominating my thoughts. We had some good friends staying with us for the first few days after my return, and they – together with Tim – helped me to debrief, letting me tell some of the stories of my trip over a few bottles of good shiraz. The evening after they left, however, when Tim and the dog had both fallen asleep, I was totally alone, and I cried hard. I remembered Denis Glennon's tortured face, and the pain sat heavily within me.

***

Tim's daily routine now included monitoring the live media feed from the ongoing court proceedings, and reporting to me anything that he thought would be of interest. I was astonished when he told me that Telstra's payroll manager had said in court not only that Telstra had no record of Edwards' attack on me or of his subsequent conviction on that charge, but that the company had promoted Edwards to a grade 2 technician just one year after the attack, and to a senior telecommunications technician two years later.

I found this information extremely distressing, and quite disturbing considering that Edwards had carried out his attack on me *while at work – in uniform, representing his employer* – that he had been serving a sentence of probation for the eighteen months following the attack, and that he had been ordered to attend a sexual offenders' program and counselling as part of this sentence. Surely reports from at least some of these activities must have been provided to his employer. Why did they have no record of any of them? I wondered whether

Telstra had any record of the meeting that Dave and I had attended. And I wondered, again, just who that Telecom representative was who had advocated so strongly for 'young Bradley'.

My concerns were validated when I listened to the *West Australian*'s podcast from the day I'd given my evidence. As legal affairs editor Tim Clarke and veteran reporters Natalie Bongiorno and Alison Fan were discussing the day's events, they expressed their own amazement that a man convicted of an assault while on the job had not in fact lost his job. They gave voice to the very same total disbelief that I had felt when the Telecom manager had advocated for Edwards, and again a week or so later when I'd found out he'd only been charged with common assault. In trying to understand just what had occurred 'behind the scenes' following Edwards' assault on me, Clarke mentioned the probability of a witness statement having been provided to the magistrate prior to his sentencing. But I did not remember providing any such statement. Nobody had asked me. It had been taken out of my hands, had indeed all happened 'behind the scenes'.

As more of the facts surrounding Edwards' 1990 attack on me were becoming publicly known – including to me – my outrage and my anxiety were soaring. A week or so after I'd travelled to Perth to give my own evidence, a statement of evidence from the security guard who'd been on duty at Hollywood Hospital on the day that Edwards had attacked me was read out to the court. Because I'd been in shock immediately after the attack, I had no clear memory of the security guard's attendance and I don't remember speaking with him. But in his statement, he confirmed that he had seen me, obviously distressed, being comforted by another staff member. When he then went into the social work office, his statement said, Edwards was sitting on a chair with his head in his hands, muttering to himself. When the security guard questioned him about what had just occurred, Edwards reportedly said to him: 'I don't know why I did it. I don't know what came over me. I just grabbed her and tried to drag her into the toilet cubicle.' It suddenly became clear to me then that this statement would have been given to the police at the time of the attack and, as I read the details, I was overcome with rage.

I had known at the time, without a shadow of a doubt, what Edwards had been trying to do to me. I had known that I was fighting for my life. But it was chilling to hear this clear, detailed confirmation that he had in fact *admitted* at the time that he was attempting to abduct me, to drag me into the toilet. And he had had cable ties in his pocket. And he had been ordered to attend a program for sexual offenders. And still he had only been charged with common assault. 'Furious' doesn't do my response justice. What had the police who'd dealt with the attack been thinking?

I stewed over these facts for a few days, and then decided to call Brad Hollingsworth. The last contact we'd had had been by text message, the day after I'd returned from Perth, when he had thanked me for attending court and giving my evidence under what he was sure must have been 'extremely difficult and emotional circumstances'.

It was the end of a long week when I called, and he sounded tired but also wired with energy. We began by catching up on events since we'd last been in touch. He told me that, because I had given my evidence in person in the courtroom, the woman who had been assaulted by Edwards in Huntingdale in 1988 had felt encouraged to do the same, and I was gratified to hear this.

I then told him of my shock and disbelief at Telstra's lack of records of Edwards' attack on me, and at its revelation that he had been promoted soon afterwards. For me, I explained to Brad, this revelation brought back all of the anger I had felt at the time of the meeting with the Telecom manager, and the distress I had experienced when I'd found out that Edwards had been charged with common assault. I also told him about the podcast, and how the presenters had echoed my own disbelief. He listened carefully, and then responded: 'Well, it looks as though Telstra has got some explaining to do at some point. They seem to have been very unforthcoming with information. Perhaps you need to tell your story.'

* * *

That weekend was difficult for me. I knew from the media reports that there was some public interest in the details of Edwards' prior conviction for assaulting me. Like me, people were trying to understand exactly what circumstances might have contributed to enabling his escalation from convicted assaulter to confessed rapist to alleged killer. I knew I had some information that might help flesh out the story, but it seemed that Telstra was denying all knowledge of the assault, and Dave was no longer alive to corroborate my version of events. I was also very apprehensive about speaking to the media. If and when I decided to tell my full story, I wanted to do it in my own way, in my own time, on my own terms. But I felt so angry, so anxious to set the record straight, and my mind kept going round and round. I didn't know what to do.

On Sunday night, I finally bit the bullet and sent an email to the chief of staff at the *West Australian*. I told her who I was and said that I had been surprised to hear that Telstra had no record of the 1990 Hollywood Hospital attack on Bradley Edwards' file, because my recollection was that someone at Telstra definitely *had* known about the attack at the time, and that if the *West Australian*'s legal affairs editor Tim Clarke would like to speak with me about this issue, he was welcome to email me back.

Waiting to hear back from the newspaper, I became increasingly anxious that I had done the wrong thing, that I would in some way impede the progress of the trial if I spoke to the media, that my actions might have some kind of damaging outcome for the families of the victims, that it was not my role to instigate this discussion, that I would get into trouble – that I shouldn't be making a fuss.

And so I messaged Brad Hollingsworth again, to tell him what I had done and to ask if he could answer some of my questions, allay some of my fears. He called me back a few days later, this time in a different mood from our previous contact. He began the conversation with, 'I know what I said before but, having given things more thought ...' and went on to explain that the information I had would only become significant if Edwards was found guilty – if it turned out that he was in fact the Claremont serial killer. If not, then his attack on me years earlier could be regarded merely as an assault, a significant incident nonetheless, but one that Telstra had forgotten to – or chosen not to – put on record. The DPP now wanted to focus on the mammoth task of presenting the relevant evidence directly relating to the murders that the police had gathered over the past decades, and they did not want any distractions. Katy would be my liaison person until the end of the trial. The message was very clear: this was not the time to make a fuss.

I fully understood the need for the DPP to now focus solely on bringing Edwards to justice for the murders. Thanking Brad for his call, and wishing him good luck with the rest of the trial and a Merry Christmas, I also felt some relief that this was not the time for my story to be made public. At the same time, however, I felt a nagging sense of once again being stifled, silenced. Whether or not Edwards was found guilty of the murders would not alter the fact that his attack on me had been violent and sexually motivated, that is had involved attempted abduction, had caused me injury and trauma, and almost certainly had not resulted in an appropriate charge. As it turned out, his fingerprints had already been on file from the earlier Huntingdale offences and, five years after he'd attacked me, he would go on to brutally abduct, assault and rape a seventeen-year-old woman in Karrakatta Cemetery. What happened at Hollywood Hospital had never been merely a case of common assault.

As my call with Brad ended, an email came through. It was from Tim Clarke from the *West Australian*. It was validating, respectful, and he was interested in my information. I replied, telling him that, on reflection and after speaking further with the DPP, I felt that at this stage I could not yet talk about my experience. I added that I would be happy to discuss things with him once the trial was finished. He understood. I was sure we would have more contact.

***

Over the next few weeks, as the trial approached its scheduled two-week break for Christmas 2019, the number of witnesses called by the prosecution surpassed the one-hundred mark. The evidence being presented now focused specifically on the disappearances of Sarah, Jane and Ciara. The court heard a description of 'bloodcurdling screams' heard by a witness in Mosman Park not long after Sarah had hailed a taxi that was unable to locate her when it arrived. There were witnesses who reported having seen the women before their disappearances, witnesses who had seen a man driving a Telstra van in the area at the time, witnesses who had been offered a lift by someone driving a Telstra vehicle, and some who had accepted such a lift late at night. I thought about how they must now be feeling, how they must be counting their blessings that their lift did not turn into something far more sinister.

Further details were also revealed about the DNA and fibre evidence that the prosecution asserted linked Edwards to Jane's and Ciara's bodies. Both young women had been found with tiny blue polyester fibres on their hair or clothing that matched with fibres taken from the Telstra uniforms worn by Edwards at the time of the attacks. Grey polypropylene fibres identical to those from the car that Edwards had driven at the time were also found on Jane's body. It was predicted that the defence would focus on strongly challenging this evidence, and I had no doubt that some of the details that would be argued over would be exceedingly difficult for the families of the murdered women to hear.

4

In January 2020, my brother and his wife travelled down from New South Wales for a week to help celebrate my seventieth birthday. As we dined out with the family, I looked at them and wondered where all the years had gone, how many more celebrations we would have together.

My preoccupation with the trial had underscored all of our activities and intruded into our Christmas festivities. It had woven an ever-present thread of anxiety through everything I did, feeling like slightly ominous, unfinished business. As we moved into February, I realised that Tim and I had also had visitors staying with us almost continuously since mid-October the previous year and, despite all the joy this had brought us, we were both now feeling tired and a little grumpy.

* * *

The trial had resumed in early January, and I was keeping pace with proceedings thanks to the live feed from the courtroom and the media reports streaming out regularly from the West. As expected, the focus was now on forensics. Out of respect for the victims' families, Justice Hall had ruled that any visual material considered 'sensitive' could be seen only by those who absolutely needed to view it – basically himself, the prosecution and defence teams, and the accused. Video evidence was presented to them from behind temporarily erected privacy screens, showing the sites where the murdered women's bodies had been found, and the bodies themselves. This was accompanied by detailed verbal descriptions that could be heard by all present, outlining the processes and procedures used to properly manage and examine this evidence.

On day thirty-one of the trial, at the request of the victims' families, a temporary suppression order was issued banning the publication of any details relating to the post-mortem examinations conducted on the bodies of Jane and Ciara, the reports on which were to be read out in court that day. On day thirty-two, Seven West Media, while respecting the order, requested that it be lifted in the interests of accurate reporting. Justice Hall agreed, saying he was 'uncomfortable censoring the press'. And so the previous day's evidence was able to be made public. Over the next few days, further details from the reports written by the forensic pathologists who had conducted the autopsies on the murdered women were revealed in court.

Throughout this horrendous recounting of the discovery and examination of the murdered women's bodies, Edwards was observed by those in court to be calmly watching as disturbing details were presented and discussed. He took notes, often averting his eyes when graphic material was displayed, and he showed no overt emotion. I wondered whether he had been prescribed some kind of calming medication, effectively numbed to the horrors he was observing – horrors that he himself was on trial for.

On 3 February, the state's new police commissioner, Chris Dawson, made his first visit to the court. This visit coincided with the completion of a detailed presentation of evidence relating to DNA testing carried out on Ciara Glennon's fingernails. Initial testing done of one fingernail in 1997 had not shown the presence of any male DNA. In 2003 and 2004, samples were sent to New Zealand for more advanced testing, but again only showed Ciara's own DNA. In 2008 Mr Dawson, then deputy commissioner, had the Macro Task Force look at more advanced DNA testing technology that at the time was being used only in the UK. Four nail samples from Ciara Glennon were sent to the government-owned forensics laboratory used by the courts in Britain and, when tested, were found to contain the DNA of a then unknown male. In 2009, Australian company PathWest ran these

UK DNA results through its existing database and found that they matched samples previously taken from the Karrakatta rape victim. But at that time the perpetrator of that rape was also unknown, and there was still no match with any identified person on the Australian DNA database. Eight years later, with the help of ever-improving technology, further matches were made with DNA samples taken from the Huntingdale kimono that had been stored in police evidence archives for twenty-five years. Fingerprints taken from a related Huntingdale break-in were then matched with those taken from the person who had been charged with – and confessed to – attacking me at Hollywood Hospital in 1990: Bradley Robert Edwards.

Over three days, a senior PathWest scientist explained in detail the processes and procedures used during the DNA analysis prior to the UK testing, and then in the transfer of the samples to the UK. Initially, her evidence appeared to preclude any possibility of contamination from any other samples in the laboratory, and it was hard to imagine how the defence would be able to refute what seemed to be incontrovertible proof that Edwards was at least present when Ciara died.

As the week went on, however, Mr Yovich proceeded to attack the credibility of every witness, every process and procedure used to collect and analyse that precious DNA data, sowing as many seeds of doubt as he was able to in defence of his client. He even raised the possibility of another suspect – a now deceased man who had been unfairly hounded by WA police for many years in their now obviously misguided investigations into the Claremont murders.

* * *

As I walked with Maisie in the park, I tried to shake off the apprehensive feeling that had overtaken me after this latest development in the trial. I sat down on a bench and looked at the trees, dense and heavy with leaves that would soon start to fall away as the seasons changed. Maisie looked up at me quizzically, no doubt wondering why I had interrupted our walk, and I noted her greying muzzle and changing shape. Three years before, when Edwards had been arrested, she'd been in the prime of her life, and I realised suddenly that we were both now on the home straight.

I knew that my peace of mind in the final decade or so of my life would be affected by the outcome of this trial. I desperately wanted Edwards to be convicted, to be found guilty, for justice to be done – because I knew in my heart that he was a killer. For those few interminable seconds some thirty years earlier, I had felt his hands upon me, I had known his rage and his brutality, and when I'd looked into his molten, dark eyes I had seen nothing but a strange disassociation that I didn't understand.

5

In March 2020, Tim and I were looking forward to a family Easter, with everyone due to fly in to Hobart for a week together. Tickets had been booked, arrangements made. At the beginning of March, however, like something out of a futuristic sci-fi movie, media outlets worldwide started reporting on a new virus that had first been identified in Wuhan in China but was spreading rapidly – a potentially deadly new form of coronavirus that was starting to appear in countries all over the world.

As the news spread, local supermarkets quickly became low on toilet rolls and long-life milk. Tinned produce disappeared rapidly, and our streets, usually buzzing with overseas students from the nearby university, became almost deserted. As the situation developed, I wondered whether we should continue with our Easter plans, particularly given that Tim's MS would put him at greater risk of serious illness in the event of any exposure to the virus. At that time, however, Tasmania still seemed a long way away from what was just the beginning of the global COVID-19 pandemic.

Darwin had completely sold out of face masks and hand sanitiser, and my daughter Jo was reluctant to fly from her home there to Hobart with her toddler unless they could be properly protected. A visit to our local chemist yielded some children's masks, but they too had sold out of adult masks and hand sanitiser; so had the other two chemists in our area, as well as the main medical suppliers in Hobart. I managed to buy some rubbing alcohol and aloe vera gel so I could make some hand sanitiser myself, and I scrounged around our cupboards and found a few adult masks to send her. But I was starting to understand that we would probably not be seeing our family for a while.

In the end we cancelled our Easter gathering, as Australia closed its borders to international travel and Tasmania went into virtual lockdown, with all incoming travellers required to self-quarantine for two weeks in an attempt to control the spread of the virus. Worldwide reports came in by the hour describing the horrors facing countries such as Italy, which was hit hard by the pandemic. As the death rate across the globe rose, everyone was struggling to retain some sort of equilibrium amid the general feeling of subdued panic.

* * *

By all reports, it seemed that the trial would carry on despite the massive upheaval being caused by the virus. Because there was no jury to consider, it seemed it might just be possible to continue. Sanitising and physical distancing protocols would be implemented, witnesses would be able to give their evidence by video link, and court visitors would be discouraged. It was also likely that the trial schedule would be reduced by a couple of days a week, in order to limit the time everyone had to spend together in the courtroom. Justice Hall seemed determined to do all in his power to bring the trial to its proper conclusion despite the overwhelming circumstances occurring in the wider world.

* * *

My growing concern about the pandemic was underscored by another source of unease about the trial. The defence team had now formally raised the argument of possible contamination of some of the prosecution's DNA evidence. The professional conduct and integrity of long-term pathology laboratory employees were being questioned, and examples were provided that suggested negligence in the handling of key forensic evidence in this and other criminal cases. Reading the media reports, it was becoming harder to separate factual evidence directly relevant to this case from theoretical red herrings strategically thrown in by the defence in order to sow seeds of doubt in the minds of both the public and – more importantly – Justice Hall.

As the live feed from the courtroom and the daily podcasts from the *West Australian* continued, I listened to details about the collection and analysis of the crucial fibre evidence that linked Edwards' clothes and car to the bodies of both Jane and Ciara. Expert witnesses had testified that fibres found on the victims' bodies matched those of the seat inserts, the boot and the floor of the work car that Edwards had been driving at the time of the murders. Further connections had been made between fibres from Telstra-regulation workwear in the 1990s and fibres found on the bodies of Jane and Ciara and on the clothes of the seventeen-year-old woman who had been raped by Edwards in Karrakatta Cemetery in 1995. With each witness, the links became clearer, and the odds of mere coincidence seemed to lessen, the inferences of real connection strengthened. The UK DNA expert who had first found Edwards' DNA under Ciara Glennon's fingernails described the defence's suggestion that it had got there through contamination as 'implausible', 'highly unlikely' and 'unreasonable', his unequivocal testimony reinforcing the 'high' likelihood that DNA transfer had occurred while Ciara had bravely fought for her life. Previous evidence relating to Telstra cars seen in the vicinity of the murders was now making more sense, the jigsaw pieces starting to fall into place, and it all seemed pretty damning. I had to continually remind myself to remain objective, to watch the process as it unfolded and to trust that Justice Hall, in his final deliberations, would be able to separate the wheat from the chaff.

There was a break scheduled for the Easter period, and then the prosecution would call its final witnesses, mostly relating to more detailed fibre evidence, before the defence was called to present its own case. We were coming close to the final chapter.

* * *

Because of my age and Tim's health, we were classified as particularly vulnerable to the virus, so we cancelled all supports coming into the home. Traci, our friend and cleaner, became our shopper, dropping by weekly to leave bags of groceries on our doorstep, which I would disinfect before I took them inside. I did the same with all other deliveries, including mail. Stocking up on our regular prescription medications, I worried that basic supplies would run out, that our health services would be unable to cope. As my daughter Martha dropped a few things off to us, she maintained an appropriate distance, and I missed our hugs. How on earth would we manage for months like this?

Stuck at home, everything started to take on a drawn-out, dream-like quality. Hunkered down and stripped of outside demands and responsibilities, our routine changed. Things became simpler. Morning coffee was now a ritual, something to be appreciated, and we sat together again over afternoon tea to listen to the daily trial podcasts and watch replays of *Antiques Roadshow*. We called and messaged our family and friends regularly, particularly those living alone. When Traci came by to drop off the shopping, carefully keeping her distance, ready to move on to her next appointment, I tried to engage her in conversation, to keep her there with me just a little longer.

Meanwhile, Maisie had just been given the sack from doggy day care. Well, not exactly – it was a little more civilised than that. She had been going to the same one in Hobart every Friday since she was six months old, and it was her favourite place in the world – or it had been, until recently. Every Friday morning for seven years I had dropped her off and, her tail up and straining at the leash, she had dragged me inside so she could play happily with her friends all day, before coming home in the late afternoon completely sated to snore contentedly on the couch. But the time had come when she was starting to slow down, so I was saddened but not completely surprised when the lovely owner called me early one Friday afternoon to say: 'Can you come and pick Maisie up please, Wendy? She's bitten another dog.' It wasn't too serious, thank goodness. She'd got involved in a melee and bitten another dog's tail, but he was okay. Nevertheless, it was clear that as she aged, and had gradually less energy, she was beginning to feel a little overwhelmed and perhaps irritable at all the stimuli. I knew just how she felt.

As daylight saving ended and the temperature dropped, the nights closed in more quickly, we wound our clocks back and it felt like we were heading into hibernation. Moving into April and with Easter approaching, it really hit home that we might not see our family and friends for a long time, and I felt unbearably sad.

6

By early May, Hobart was in full lockdown. With more than two hundred reported cases and thirteen deaths on the island, Tasmania's state government, mindful of our elderly population and relatively limited infrastructure, was taking a very cautious approach, and the restrictions were expected to remain in place for some weeks, if not months.

Tim and I had by now settled into our new, somewhat restricted routine, which I think perhaps was easier for us than some. Our daily exercise revolved around walking the dog, and we were so grateful that Tim, thanks to the NDIS, now had an electric wheelchair – our isolation would have been much more difficult if he had been totally confined to the house. Although we missed our regular family, friend and community contact, my daughters all provided lots of support from their respective distances, and rarely more than a few days passed without a cherished call from a little one in Perth or Darwin.

There were also nightly catch-up photos and comments from our six-year-old granddaughter in Tasmania. Her father, our son-in-law Evan, had his birthday during this period. In a sad coincidence, Ev also has MS. We'd first met him in Edinburgh thirteen years ago, when Tim and I had been visiting Martha. They had just met, and she was in love. But there was something not right with Ev's health, she said; she thought he might have MS. She invited him to dinner with us and, after he'd left, said, 'What do you think, Mum and Tim?' As if we would know. And we did.

Martha had then embarked on her long journey of helping Ev and his family to accept his diagnosis. When it became too difficult for them all to face, she brought him to Tasmania. She is remarkable. She, too, has had her struggles, and it has been hard to watch her give up her career as a social worker to care for this man whom she brought here all the way from Scotland. Like Tim, Evan is strong, dealing stoically with the increasing and unpredictable ravages that this disease inflicts on his body. Our granddaughter has a strong bond with her father – he was her main carer when she was little and her mother was working – and that will surely stand her in good stead throughout her life.

Normally for Ev's birthday we would have a family gathering, with something deliciously unhealthy for dinner accompanied by a bit of Scottish banter, all washed down with a beer or two before they piled back into their car for the twenty-minute drive home. But that wasn't possible this year. It was 2020 and Tasmania, like the rest of Australia, was in lockdown. And so we video-called Ev and sang 'Happy Birthday', trying to sound jolly and happy and supportive from afar. We told him that his present was on its way, that its delivery might be delayed due to the massive increase in people buying online now that they felt unsafe in shops. He was, as always, gracious and thankful.

***

When the trial resumed after the Easter break, an hours-long videorecording of Edwards' interview with police following his arrest was played in court, with Justice Hall making it clear that this evidence was not for release to the general public. Present during the playing of the video were family members of the murdered women, the other living victims – and the parents of Bradley Edwards. I imagined that the families and victims were hoping that this recording might help them to gain some understanding of the man whom they believed had caused them such unspeakable trauma and grief, had affected their lives in so many ways. But I could not even begin to imagine what Edwards' parents were thinking as they listened to the recording of their son talking calmly with police after his arrest.

As Tim and I followed the live feed from the court, I felt frustrated that I was so far away. I wanted to be there in the courtroom. I wanted to hear Edwards' voice, his words, his stories – his lies. It was as if he had two modes in that interview: affable and chatty, very forthcoming when he was talking about his home life and his family, then flat, even terse, as he repeatedly politely and quietly told the detectives he had no knowledge of the Huntingdale assault or the Karrakatta Cemetery rape – both of which he would later confess to having committed – or of the Claremont killings. I listened, desperately wanting to watch the actual video so that I could see his body language, his reactions as the questions and the evidence of the crimes were put to him.

As the trial was progressing, the complexities of the forensic evidence on which it hinged were becoming increasingly apparent. For the past month the proceedings had been dominated by what was being referred to as the 'critical fibre evidence' that provided a proven forensic link between the two confirmed murder victims and the rape victim, the latter a crime that Edwards had admitted to perpetrating. A forensic fibres expert spent days on the stand detailing each of the ninety-eight blue and grey fibres collectively found on the victims' hair and clothing, explaining when and where they had been found and how they compared to fibres taken from Edwards' former work car and Telstra uniforms. An internationally renowned fibre expert from the UK then provided his own detailed analysis of all the fibre evidence. He was extremely critical of the way the evidence had been handled by police and forensic pathologists, maintaining that valuable evidence had been lost in the process. He did tell the court, however, that he would not expect to see the particular combinations of fibres that had been found on the bodies of Jane and Ciara if the women had not been in Edwards' car. Also of great significance was his conclusion that, during the various forensic processes, appropriate precautions had been taken to avoid contamination, ensuring that the chance of any contamination was very remote. Overall, his evidence added more support to the prosecution's case.

As the prosecution's presentation of this crucial evidence drew to a close, I was left wondering just how the defence would attempt to persuade the court that Edwards' work clothes and car were in fact not the sources of those fibres found on the bodies of the murdered women.

Later that evening, I listened to the podcast of the court reporters dissecting the day's events. Reporter Alison Fan sounded puzzled as she made some observations about Edwards' continual steadfast denials during the original police interview. She felt that, on the video, there was little discernible difference in his affect when he talked about the crimes compared to when he talked about his family. Only when the DNA evidence was put to him did he show any emotion, then seeming a little overwhelmed and surprised, but still never wavering in his denials. His mantra seemed to be: 'It wasn't me. I don't know. I wish I could help you.' Alison then drew some comparisons with his behaviour in the courtroom during the long months of the trial, including his odd lack of reaction as various witnesses, even victims, had taken the stand. And then she said something that resonated so strongly with me, and things started to fall into place: 'It's like he was in another dimension.'

All at once I was drawn back yet again to those terrifying few moments of his attack on me, feeling the frightening force with which he'd suddenly grabbed me from behind and dragged me on my chair towards the toilet area. You know when someone is serious about hurting you. I knew that his rage, in those moments, was murderous. But the immediate aftermath was different. As I broke free and his hands dropped to his sides and we briefly looked directly at each other, his gaze was unfocused, dark and vacant, almost like he was surprised to see me there. No wonder it was so difficult for anyone to understand.

* * *

When the prosecution finally concluded its case, after more than six months of meticulously weaving together detailed expert evidence and firsthand witness accounts into a strong and compelling argument, its closing remarks were brief. In summing up, Carmel Barbagallo dropped the 'emotional upset' argument that had asserted a causal link between Edwards' emotional state and each of the attacks. But she maintained that, when his first wife had left him, he had then had opportunity to perpetrate the murders undetected, which still showed a clear link between all the crimes, when considered alongside the propensity and other evidence.

To my astonishment, the defence then took just minutes to present its own case. Barrister Paul Yovich told the court that the only evidence he wished to submit was a document outlining the maximum temperatures for the City of Gosnells in 1996. While its purpose was a mystery to me at the time, I have since learned that this information was tendered as an argument against the veracity of a prosecution witness' recollections of Edwards' whereabouts on a particular day of that year, which the witness remembered as being particularly hot but which the defence asserted had not been. Justice Hall then asked Edwards whether he wished to give evidence in his own defence. Edwards declined, the defence closed its case, and Justice Hall adjourned the trial until 8 June, when the prosecution and the defence would each give their closing addresses.

I was stunned. I had fully expected the defence to call its own experts, to draw on its own witnesses – to present its own case. It felt like a huge anticlimax, and I could only imagine that everyone else following the trial must be feeling the same.

7

The weeks leading up to the closing addresses were quiet from a media perspective, with little coverage of the trial from the West. Hobart was moving into its fourth winter since Edwards' arrest. Having been in hibernation for months due to the COVID-19 pandemic, as Tasmania moved into its second week of no new cases and no community transmission I began to cautiously venture out, schedule certain appointments, visit friends and invite family to dinner. But it felt strange, different. We were all wondering just what would happen when the state borders eventually reopened. How would we remain safe when visitors started to come from overseas again?

The weather at that time was magnificent, a reminder of why we had moved to Hobart. The skies were cloudless, the air crisp, the sun warm on your face with no cold wind demanding a beanie when you walked. My anxiety had by now manifested in a need to walk further and further on my daily outings with Maisie, and so she often seemed a little achy at the end of the day. Together we discovered new parks and tracks, some bringing back memories of bushwalking with small children in the Perth hills many years ago. My walks, like my dreams, had now become filled with memories, some happy, some sad.

At around this time I joined a dementia prevention research study being conducted by the University of Tasmania that aimed to increase our understanding of who is most at risk of dementia and how that risk might be mitigated. There was a series of assessment forms for participants to complete, about our health, our habits. I was as honest, as accurate as I could be and, when I received some feedback, I was happy to read that I was considered to be at low risk. Except for one area. When the trial was over, I would cut down on my evening wine intake.

But for now I was cutting myself some slack.

***

The closing addresses of the trial were delayed somewhat when Carmel Barbagallo became unwell. Initially the postponement was just for one day but, as the prosecutor began attempting to give her address over a temperamental video-link connection from her home, she was coughing and obviously ill. The court was as packed as COVID-19 restrictions would allow, with the victims' families and other living victims in attendance but, in the interests of ensuring a fair trial, Justice Hall suggested a further week's postponement.

The following day, newspaper headlines from Western Australia captured the beginnings of the prosecution's closing remarks that Carmel Barbagallo had so far managed to relay, with one front page reading: '25 REASONS WHY THIS MAN IS THE CLAREMONT KILLER'. The two-page spread that followed went on to neatly outline in numbered points much of the evidence that the prosecution had presented over the past six months, focusing specifically on fibre and DNA evidence, opportunity and propensity. It was a clear, concise and damning introduction to the prosecution's closing statement, which would be further detailed the following week when court finally resumed.

***

During the break in court proceedings, an unexpected phone call brought even more angst, mixed feelings and confusion into my life, adding further stress to the long ordeal of the past few years.

Since that very first call from Katy just before Christmas 2016, I had felt a continuous internal battled between a strong need to be heard, a feeling of responsibility to tell what had happened, and a sometimes-overwhelming internal pressure not to make a fuss. For three-and-a-half years I had also been living with an underlying sense of unease that my story would one day become public, that people would want to know exactly what had happened that day at Hollywood Hospital, and I wanted to be the one in control of that story when it did eventually come out. My disquiet had escalated with each new reference to the attack in court, and was exacerbated by repeated warnings from the DPP that the media might well be interested.

One evening Maisie and I had just returned from a brisk late-afternoon walk. It was cold, the skies already closing in for another winter night. At home, the kettle on for a warming cuppa, Tim was busy in the kitchen preparing something delicious that smelled of cumin and mustard seeds. Our landline rang, but the caller ID showed a number that was unknown to us and so, assuming it would be from a call centre somewhere in a faraway land, we let it go to voicemail. There was a brief silence after the beep, and then a slightly hesitant voice said: 'It's Nick Greenaway here from *60 Minutes*. I wanted to speak with Wendy Davis. Can you please call me back when it's convenient?'

Tim and I looked at each other. My heart was jumping and sinking at the same time. Here was a real chance for me to tell my story, but oh! *60 Minutes*! Such a huge fuss!

For twenty-four hours I deliberated over whether to call back. I wasn't ready. I knew that the exposure, the stress of publicly telling my story would have negative consequences on my body, my emotions, my life. Already I could feel the adrenaline, the fight-or-flight impulses, precursors to a big health crash. Did I really want to relive the whole traumatic event so publicly? But I also knew that, for me, this was unfinished business. I was still angry, still traumatised. If I could finally let it all out, if I could just explain what had happened, if I could feel that people were actually listening to me, really hearing me, understanding what had happened – *believing* me – then perhaps I would be able to let it all go.

And so I sent Nick a message. When he called me back, he still sounded hesitant: 'I'm not sure if you're the Wendy Davis we're after ...' he began. 'I think I am the Wendy Davis you're after,' I told him.

We chatted for nearly an hour, and I think I said a great deal more than he had expected. He is not from Western Australia, and it was clear to me that he did not know the Claremont story in detail. He was trying to work out just what had happened in 1990: had the police actually been negligent or was it all just a tragic story, with misjudgements made at the time but only apparent now in hindsight? I told him that I had been writing my story and would like it told, that I would send it to him in its raw and unfinished form so that he could understand.

As the conversation drew to a close, he said that, if I did agree to an interview, he would send Liam Bartlett from Perth to speak to me. Suddenly it all became just a little more personal as, smiling to myself, I told him that I actually knew Liam from many years ago. 'Ask him if he remembers Wendy and John Davis, who lived next door to him in Medina when he was just a little blond-headed boy,' I said.

Nick sent me a text half an hour later: 'Spoke to Liam – he is absolutely gobsmacked it's you ... says John was friends with his older brother and sister?'

Telling Tim the story later, I wondered aloud at the coincidence, and I thought that maybe, just maybe, it would all be okay, that perhaps it would be a good thing to do. To tell my story.

* * *

The day after that call, my feelings were very mixed. In the morning, my mobile flashed with a call from Liam Bartlett. His voice was booming.

'Wendy!' he roared.

'Liam!' I answered, smiling to myself once again at the smallness of the world. We chatted over some shared memories, caught up a little on family news and agreed that, if COVID-19 restrictions allowed, we would meet soon; if not, he would interview me over Zoom.

Later that day, trying to process this unexpected development, I felt exhausted. What was happening felt overwhelming, almost out of my control, like a truck hurtling off a cliff. The excitement that I'd initially felt about having a chance to finally tell my story was almost completely overshadowed by the fear of doing so. I wondered what the next few weeks would bring.

As the days passed, my fear of talking publicly dominated my every waking moment. I worried about what people would think, whether they would understand just how violent and strange the attack had been, whether anyone would even care about the aftermath of it, the involvement of the Telecom manager, the lesser charge, my anger and my trauma – whether it would all just seem as though I was making a huge fuss about nothing.

I emailed Nick Greenaway to say that I had reconsidered, that I didn't think it was appropriate for me to speak out, that I wanted to maintain my privacy, that I didn't want to upset anyone. His reply was disappointed but gentle, understanding and validating, and he left it open for me to reconsider again.

And, over the next week, I did. I would speak with Liam. I would tell my story.

* * *

When court finally resumed, Carmel Barbagallo was back in top form. Clearly summarising what she maintained was irrefutable evidence that Edwards was indeed the Claremont serial killer, she focused first on the DNA and fibre evidence, citing her expert witnesses' view that Edwards was clearly forensically linked to his victims. She reiterated that a renowned forensic scientist had confirmed that the DNA found under Ciara Glennon's fingernails was eighty million times more likely to be from Edwards than anyone else, and that fibres found on the bodies of both Jane and Ciara had been matched with fibres from the car that Edwards had driven at the time of the murders and with work clothes of the type that he had worn. She then recapitulated her compelling, concise rebuttals of the defence's suggestions of contamination of this evidence – which, she said, showed 'desperation' on the part of the defence. She also urged Justice Hall to see that the Karrakatta rape, to which Edwards had now admitted, had in fact been an intended murder that was interrupted, a precursor to the three murders that followed over the next eighteen months, that Edwards had a propensity to attack lone, vulnerable women, and that he had created opportunities to do so by driving around Claremont late at night. She left, it would seem, little room for argument, and I wondered what Mr Yovich would say when it was his turn to sum up the defence case.

Edwards' lawyer began his summary, as expected, with a focus on the possibility of contamination of the DNA evidence. He cited a number of 'bad practice' events that he said had occurred in the handling and analysis of the evidence, he questioned the miniscule amount of DNA found under Ciara's fingernails, and he emphasised the fact that nine stray hairs had also been found on her body whose source had not been identified. As he continued his summation, my anxiety increased with each sentence. He argued in detail against every piece of evidence that had been presented by the prosecution, and I was reminded that Paul Yovich was indeed one of the best defence lawyers in Western Australia. Towards the end of his summary I felt a sudden surge of apprehension, a real fear that there might not be enough evidence to convict Edwards 'beyond reasonable doubt', and my whole body started to ache. My spine, my feet, my ribs, my breastbone, my shoulders, my fingers, my hips. It was unlike anything I had ever experienced, and it was accompanied by an all-pervasive anxiety. I just wanted it to be over.

***

The trial finished on 25 June 2020, with Justice Hall announcing that he would bring down his verdict on 24 September. I was overcome with conflicting emotions. Mr Yovich's dogged determination to question every shred, every witness, every fibre had left my head swirling with unanswered questions, and I wondered what sense Justice Hall would make of it all. I desperately hoped the trial would prove to have been worth all the effort. I hoped Bradley Robert Edwards would be found guilty of murder.

8

By now it was midwinter and the weather in Hobart was absolutely freezing, with maximum temperatures hovering between nine and eleven degrees for weeks. The sun struggled for a few hours every morning to break through the oppressive cloud cover, but it never quite got there and eventually it gave up. Despite the weather, Maisie and I, both rugged up against the cold, headed out every morning for our daily walk, albeit a little more slowly now that her stiff little legs no longer moved as quickly as they once did.

Some positive things were happening during this time. I had discovered that the dementia research project that I was involved in had begun a study on the impacts of university education on dementia risk, and was offering participants a broad range of courses at the University of Tasmania free of charge. I had long been interested in learning Mandarin and, when I looked at the courses on offer, beginners Mandarin was included, commencing either in the second semester of that year or the first semester of the following year. I knew, of course, that it would have to be the following year for me, since there wouldn't be enough room in my life until the trial was completely over and the verdict had been handed down. But it was the first time in a long while that I could even see something beyond the verdict, and that in itself felt good.

In early July, Tim and I booked a week away for late August, in a house a few kilometres outside the quiet seaside town of Penguin, overlooking Bass Strait. It would be respite, something different, a change of scenery. Looking forward to the break, I could actually feel a little bit of the tension leaving my body.

It grew even colder. One night in mid-July the temperature plummeted to one degree and, as Maisie and I walked in the park the following morning, there was frost on the grass and thick, freezing mud in the hollows between the tree roots. As we walked home my toes, wet in my boots from the sodden grass, were frozen. When we arrived home Tim had coffee waiting, bless him. As I sipped from the steaming cup, my eyes strayed to the big, colourful painting on the wall above the dining table. My old friend Bill Webb – Harry, to his arty friends – had painted that. I'd met Bill more than thirty years ago, when I was working at Hollywood Hospital. He was an interesting man, a dental surgeon and artist from Sydney who'd gone looking for himself in Italy, France, the Greek islands, delving deep into religion and philosophy, growing his hair and exploring different lifestyles. He'd ended up in Montreal where, while holding an exhibition of his paintings, he was diagnosed with advanced cancer with little that could be done to help. He'd packed up and flown to Perth – having visited many years before, he felt it would be a good place to die. It was here that I met him. Through my job at Hollywood Hospital, I was Bill's counsellor and support person. Together, we found him a small flat on the top floor of a block in Fremantle, overlooking the Indian Ocean. As he became weaker, we moved his bed to the window so he could see the view. When he became too weak to live there, we moved him into the palliative care unit at the hospital. He talked – about his life, about so many things, about how grateful he was for all the care we gave him. And he had one last wish: a final art exhibition. We rearranged the furniture in the visiting area, borrowed easels, bought champagne, cheese. Afterwards he gave all his paintings away to the staff who were caring for him – all except one, which, at his request, we hung at the end of his bed so he could look at it in his final days. It represented his life – full of conflicting figures and images, vibrant with colour and suggestive of painful growth. It was that picture that I was now gazing at. I had loved that job so very much.

I found myself crying, the tears coursing unchecked down my cheeks. I couldn't stop. The pain was visceral. The feeling of grief was so overpowering that I could hardly draw breath. My tears were for all the losses – for my job, for the career that I had loved, for my sense of trust, for the lives of the murdered women, for their families, for all the victims. I cried for a long time, until I was empty, breathing, grounded. Then I washed my face. We were going out for lunch with our friend Vikki. It was her birthday.

* * *

It was nearly September – less than a month until the verdict would be handed down. News on the global spread of the pandemic had been alarming and, when I ventured out, I could feel that something had changed. People had become a little less relaxed, a little more edgy.

As the days rolled by with no noise from the West, I could also feel something changing inside me. Tim and I travelled to the north of the state for the holiday we'd booked just outside Penguin. The views from every window were calming, peaceful. They reminded me of our smallness, our insignificance next to the vast expanse of water that stretched to the horizon, indistinguishable from the sky. Maisie and I walked to the nearby dog beach every morning, and I realised that I was starting to take more notice of the things around me again – the gently increasing hum of the traffic as we moved closer to the highway, the loud chirruping of the flock of sparrows in the bushes on the corner of the street, the soft gurgling of the creek as it trickled under the bridge near the ocean. I was beginning to understand the cumulative impact that the events of the past nearly four years had had on me. I could feel myself becoming more present. Something was starting to lift off me. But the journey was not quite over yet.

* * *

A short time after we returned from our break, I received another call from Nick Greenaway and, a few weeks later, we filmed the *60 Minutes* interview. Because of the pandemic it was, of course, done by video link. In any case, the process was all new to me – I had never done anything like it before, never been interviewed by a journalist, never appeared on television. It felt exciting and terrifying, all at the same time.

At 10.30 am on the scheduled day, a local young audio technician and a cameraman brought their equipment through our back gate, rearranged our dining room and set up the laptop through which I would speak with Liam in Perth. They were respectful, friendly, but slightly reserved. I wondered what they knew of my story. As they tested the audio, a high-pitched beeping sent Maisie scurrying outside, tail between her legs. She stayed away until they were packing up.

I'm not sure how long the filming of the interview took. Liam was direct, his questions focused, and I tried to answer them clearly, but it was not easy, yet again reliving a long-ago trauma. He interrupted me sometimes, before I'd finished what I wanted to say, and I was relieved when I heard Nick's voice in the background, telling him to slow down, give me an opportunity to talk. The worst part of the experience for me was the sense underlying every word I spoke that nobody would really be interested in what I had to say – that I would in some way be in trouble for speaking out. Even after all I had been through, after telling my story in the very public forum of the Supreme Court, it was strange that this feeling of making a fuss was so deeply entrenched in me.

Later in the afternoon, when the interview itself was over, Tim and I piled into the car with Maisie and drove down the road to the park. They wanted some footage of us doing something normal, walking the dog together in the park by the river, the beautiful, majestic mountain in the background. But it didn't feel normal, it felt staged – Tim struggling with his walker, Maisie straining at the lead, desperate to run free after being cooped up inside all day. As they fiddled with their camera drone overhead and asked us to walk here and there, guided us this way and that, I felt exhausted. I was still wondering whether I was doing the right thing.

After the interview, there was contact from a Perth lawyer. She would be lodging an application to vary the suppression order on my name, so that my interview could be aired, and it would need to be accompanied by an affidavit explaining exactly why I wished for this to happen. We discussed my reasons over the phone and, when her draft of the affidavit arrived, I was amazed at its detail. It spoke of my status, my work experience, my wish to publish my story, and I wondered at the necessity of all that. And then I realised. The procedure was for my own protection. It was to assure the judge that I fully understood all the potential ramifications of my name being made public. That I was aware that other media outlets would likely be interested. That everyone would know what had happened, that people would have opinions, some of which might not resonate with my own memories and interpretations of what had happened all those years ago, that some people would even doubt the veracity of my story, my motives, that some might very well disapprove of my choosing to foreground my own story in this way.

I felt so anxious, worried, even frightened, but the filming was already done. Despite my discomfort, my fears, I was sure that the story needed to be told. I wanted it to be told.

* * *

The process of filming the interview left both Tim and me feeling very tired. Neither of us slept well for weeks afterwards. One of Tim's sisters in the West became very unwell, and he was worried, distracted. The weather in Hobart was oppressively overcast, tinged for days with a strange twilight hue. When I took Maisie for shorter walks than normal, she didn't complain – she was happy to get back home into the warm. I turned the electric blankets on after lunch and we went back to bed for afternoon naps. It was easy to slip into this habit. There were no visitors to disturb us – family and friends, like us, had settled into new, more self-contained routines.

On one such afternoon I lay in bed, listening to the faint hum of the traffic, to Tim's soft snoring as he lay sleeping beside me. He was cradling my body, and his hand twitched against my side every now and again. I wondered what he was dreaming about. I didn't sleep. I was still thinking about what might be going through the minds of the other people on this journey. Those back in the West. The Spiers family, the Rimmers and the Glennons, the other living victims, Justice Hall, Carmel Barbagallo, Paul Yovich, Brad Hollingsworth, Katy and Brendan – even Bradley Edwards himself. What were they all thinking about while we were all waiting?

After an hour or so, Tim awoke, refreshed for the afternoon. He got up and, gently pulling the blanket back up over my shoulders, tucked me in. I felt Maisie creeping up the bed, claiming the warm spot he had left. She pressed her little body into my back and I finally fell asleep.

9

On the evening of 24 September 2020, Justice Hall handed down his verdict. Bradley Robert Edwards was found guilty of the wilful murders of Jane Rimmer and Ciara Glennon. While there was not enough evidence to convict him of the murder of Sarah Spiers, Justice Hall made it clear that he thought it likely that Edwards had also murdered her. Edwards' sentence would be announced on 23 December – exactly four long years after his arrest.

* * *

The few weeks before the verdict was handed down had seen a flurry of activity, with lots of contact from the West. There was an email from Brendan, Katy's colleague at the DPP. Katy was now working on other matters, so he was checking in with me, touching base before the verdict was due to be delivered. He told me that the ABC's media liaison office had requested an interview with me, as well as with all the other living victims and families involved, and that it was entirely my decision how I would respond to this request. I thanked him for the contact, and asked him to pass on my email address to the ABC. He said he would be in contact again on the afternoon of the verdict.

There was a message from Tim Clarke from the *West Australian*, hoping for an interview after the verdict. He had been busy writing his own book about the case, *Enigma of the Dark*, and the *West* had run detailed excerpts from various chapters. Our friends and family in the West, wanting to ensure we were up to date with all the latest information on the case in the media, had sent us copies of the various articles.

Nick Greenaway sent through the draft *60 Minutes* segment, asking for my comments. I found it graphic, sad, damning. He expressed his hope that they would do my story justice, saying that their aim was to present it strongly, objectively, respectfully, truthfully. I was by now filled with trepidation, anxiously wondering how everyone would feel after the program was aired the following Sunday night.

A week or so before the verdict was due to be handed down, Tim's sister Sue called me from Perth. Since I would not be there myself, she felt strongly compelled to go to court to hear the verdict in person – to be my presence, my proxy. When she told me this, I was overcome with conflicting feelings. While I was greatly appreciative of her offer, of her caring, of her loving consideration, I worried that the overpowering atmosphere, the frenzied emotion that would no doubt fill the packed courtroom would be too much for her, as I know her to be a deep, sensitive soul. If I am honest, I also felt robbed of my own opportunity to be there. I was so far away, and the impacts of the pandemic had taken away my choice of whether to attend court for the announcement of the verdict, to perhaps gain some sense of closure in this long, long process.

Talking later over the phone with my Perth-based friend Sheila, I discovered that she, too, wanted to be present in court, to hear the verdict. Sue and Sheila had never met, but they made arrangements to meet outside the court at seven am on the day of the verdict to hear justice being delivered. For me.

***

Throughout the morning that Justice Hall handed down his verdict, Sue and Sheila provided me with an emotional link to what was happening some three thousand kilometres away on the other side of the country. They queued for hours in the chilly early morning, fended off reporters and messaged me at regular intervals with detailed updates of the proceedings. They kept me engaged and involved. Ironically, they also found common ground in their own personal tragedies, crying together later over lunch for the sadness of it all and for the relief that, for Perth, for the families, for the other living victims, for me, a significant part of this long, drawn-out, tragic story was now finally over.

From Hobart, Tim and I closely followed the live TV footage, watching the arrivals and departures of the various family members, the police and the judiciary. Reading the subsequent media descriptions of their reactions to the verdict, the sense of release that everyone felt at the end of that long exhausting journey was clear. Jane Rimmer's and Ciara Glennon's families shared sombre hugs with the prosecution, and tears of relief were shed. Sarah Spiers' family members were resigned, stoic and sad. I watched as Bradley Edwards' parents strode quickly away from the court, united in what looked to me like an angry departure. I watched all of their faces, and I felt everything.

Later that day, listening for a second time to Justice Hall's broadcast of the verdict, I could feel a little more of the tension draining from my body with every word, every sentence.

Later again, there was a call from the Perth lawyer. She had presented the application for the removal of the suppression order on my name to Justice Hall. He was not happy with the clause that retained my right to withhold permission to publish my name in the absence of my prior written permission. He didn't want me to have that power: it should be all or nothing, he said. So I said okay, let's make it all. I was terrified of what that might mean, but I pushed my fear down and, when she called back again, it was done.

* * *

By mid-October 2020, I felt as if I'd been emptied. The 'incident', which had been buried for twenty-five years and then relived repeatedly for nearly another four, had finally come spewing out. The more I realised that people were now actually listening, the more I wanted to talk. I couldn't stop myself. Because I had written it all down, because I had now relived it so many times, it just spewed forth, and I could not stop expressing my anger, my hurt, my outrage.

I told the story over and over. I'd told it to *60 Minutes*, and now I told it to the ABC, to Channel 7, to radio station 6PR and, finally, to Tim Clarke and Natalie Bongiorno for a special podcast called *Claremont: The Trial*, produced by the *West Australian*.

Ever since that first phone call from Katy – even before the arrest of Bradley Edwards for the Claremont murders – I'd been wanting to tell my story. I wanted the whole of Western Australia, the whole of Australia, to be as angry at the Western Australia Police and at Telstra as I had been all those years ago, when neither had listened to me, when they had both dealt so lightly with such a violent man – at the expense, it turned out, not only of me but of the very lives of other women.

The *60 Minutes* interview aired, and was splashed all over the front page of the *West Australian*, along with photos of me as a young woman before the attack and me now, much older, a survivor. I watched the *60 Minutes* interview, but I didn't watch or follow any of the other coverage. It wasn't for me – it was for everyone else. It was so that everyone would know what had happened.

When this outpouring was over, there was contact from family, friends, acquaintances, people I hadn't seen for years. One person who I hadn't spoken to in four decades contacted me to say he had recognised my voice in the *60 Minutes* interview before he'd recognised my name, before he'd looked up and seen it was me. He'd been in his kitchen, preparing dinner, when the familiarity of my voice had drawn him into the lounge room to watch the program. He was astonished. People contacted me to express their shock, love, care. Their calls and texts and messages filled me with validation. Finally, I felt listened to, heard, respected, held.

There were flowers from Kate, beautiful native blooms with powerful fragrances, and wine, and chocolates, things to make it all better. A friend from Western Australia asked whether I wanted copies of the *West Australian* and I said yes, but when they arrived I put them away without looking at them. Perhaps I would want to look back in years to come. Perhaps my grandchildren would be interested.

And then, totally unforeseen, there was a response from Telstra. A completely unexpected and strangely sympathetic letter arrived from a Telstra lawyer, telling me that one of the company's most senior executives would like to speak with me, and would like to tell me that they were sorry. The letter said that they were also going to issue a public apology through the media, to apologise for all the hurt that their lack of action had caused to me, both then and now, and that Telstra had not responded 'as it should have' in relation to 'the attack' on me. I was empty and numb and I could barely respond, so I declined to talk but I emailed to thank them for their acknowledgement and their assurance that things would be handled differently nowadays.

It was something, but it wasn't enough. It didn't change anything. Those young women were still dead, that teenager still raped, my life irrevocably changed, and I was so, so tired.

* * *

After the verdict was announced and the media frenzy had abated, Tim and I spent a week away on the south coast of Tasmania. Organised in a hurry, it was very nearly a disaster. My thinking was so skewed, I was so distracted, not really present. My mind was still in the West: I could not believe everything that had just happened.

I'd booked accommodation for us in White Beach. It had looked so perfect on the website: a wide balcony overlooking a beautiful expanse of deserted beach, a bath, heating, wi-fi, it was dog friendly, affordable. I had thought it would be good for us to get away, to leave it all behind for a bit, to regroup, to recover. I'd then made all our preparations on autopilot – loaded the car, tried to remember everything, food for us and for Maisie, clothes, woollens, toiletries, medications, dog bed, wheelchair, walker. As we drove out of Hobart and into the lush, green countryside, I could feel every part of my body still tensed up like a clutch of coiled springs. My adrenaline was so high, I thought that perhaps it would never dissipate. Tim, sensing my stress, said little.

As we turned off the main road and towards the bay, my tension eased a notch. I could smell the water, the fresh air, could see the wide expanse of blue. We reached the driveway to the house and looked up – and up, and up, and up. It was steep, unsealed, rocky and almost inaccessible. I stared blankly. Accessibility was usually the first thing I checked. I couldn't feel anything other than puzzlement as I looked up at that steep, rocky driveway. Tim, beside me in the car, was still being kind. I don't know what I would have done if he had been angry, disappointed, but of course he wasn't – he was kind and calm, as he always is.

I tried to manoeuvre the car up the driveway but, with the heavy electric wheelchair in the back, the wheels started spinning and I had to stop halfway. We both got out of the car and looked up at the wide balcony overhead, and I wondered how on earth Tim would get in. I didn't know what to do; I just looked. And then Tim said that he could do it, and he hauled his walker up that driveway, step by step, one foot at a time. I walked behind him in case he fell backwards, but he had this amazing, determined look on his face and I knew we would be okay.

Tim stayed in that house for the whole week, venturing out only onto the wide balcony to wave to me and Maisie as we walked along the quiet swathe of deserted beach below. We walked, and walked, and walked – so far, Tim said, that he could no longer see us in the distance, we just disappeared into the sand and the sea. I found it so hard to shake off that ever-present anxiety that had constantly ebbed and flowed in me since Edwards' arrest in 2016. Twice a day for the first three days we walked, each evening dragging ourselves back up that steep driveway, Maisie exhausted and me still alert, still waiting to come down. And then on the fourth day, it rained. Real rain. The sky darkened and it just poured down. It rained for two solid days, pounding on the tin roof and, as I sat inside looking out at it, everything started to fall away and I could breathe again.

Maisie slept for those two days, only waking up to eat. The rain finally stopped just as we were packing up to leave. As I lugged our things down the sodden muddy driveway and piled them into the car, Tim carefully negotiated his way sideways down the slope, grasping onto the side of the weatherboards for safety's sake. He climbed into the car, I buckled Maisie into her seat, and we headed for home.

When we got home, there was wine from Nick Greenaway and Liam Bartlett – good wine, as a thank you. Then Kate rang and her news was joyful: there was to be a new baby girl in the new year. Things felt almost normal again.

* * *

On 23 December 2020, Justice Stephen Hall made Western Australian judicial history when he sentenced fifty-two-year-old Bradley Robert Edwards to life imprisonment with an unprecedented forty-year non-parole period for the wilful murders of Jane Rimmer and Ciara Glennon in 1996 and 1997, respectively. He added a further twenty-four-year sentence for the 1995 rape of the seventeen-year-old woman at Karrakatta Cemetery, and six years for the assault of the young woman in her Huntingdale home in 1988.

Taking into account Edwards' age at the time of sentencing, Justice Hall acknowledged the 'high likelihood' that he would die in prison.

As the sentences were handed down, applause broke out in the courtroom's public gallery.

Epilogue

When I started writing my story, the memories tumbled out, day after day, some so vivid that they took my breath away. I'm glad now that I recorded them all. What began as fragmented notes gradually coalesced into this story. It has been an important journey for me, one that has illuminated many things about how our lives are inextricably interwoven with the lessons, the behaviours we are taught, with the values, the expectations of our community, the people who surround us.

My story did not begin with the assault at Hollywood Hospital in 1990. It began when I was born into a society whose patriarchal social institutions were originally developed within an ideology that viewed men as more important than women. Early in my life I learned that, as a female, it was easier for me to negotiate those institutions and my relationships if I didn't challenge the status quo, but conformed to the expectations of others.

My experience – the attack, the 'official' responses to it, *my* response to it, and its terrible aftermath – illustrates just what can happen when such views, such values, such teachings are given precedence in our society.

When Edwards attacked me at work in 1990 – unprovoked, violently, shockingly, terrifyingly – WA police assumed it was his first offence. They failed to fully investigate the attack, and so they failed to find that his fingerprints were already on file from the Huntingdale sexual assault. Despite the fact that his attack on me resulted in injury and trauma, despite the fact that it quite literally changed my life – caused me to abandon my newly established career, affected my closest relationships, damaged my trust in others, shook the foundations of my belief in our society, in 'the system', in justice – despite the fact that

Edwards *admitted his intention to abduct me*, police charged him only with common assault, and apparently closed the case.

Similarly, Edwards' employer – which in 1990 was still a Commonwealth Government body and not yet the privatised corporation it is today – when faced with one of its 'good workers' who had 'a good future ahead of him' being convicted of assaulting a woman *while at work*, being sentenced to two years' probation and *being ordered to attend a sexual offenders' counselling program*, responded to this situation by taking into account the fact that 'sensitive', 'fragile' 'young Bradley' was having 'relationship problems', allowed him to keep his job, to continue working with members of the public and, shortly afterwards, promoted him – twice. It also kept no record of this offence on his personnel file.

I am disappointed that to date there still has been no official acknowledgement from WA police that they could have handled things differently, no discussion about just what went wrong in 1990. Telstra's belated apology has been noted, but many unanswered questions remain about its response to that violent attack being carried out at work by one of its employees.

I believe that we still need to have these conversations – because there were in fact no real consequences for Edwards of his unprovoked violent attack on a stranger while at work. His resulting police record was minor. He retained his job, his career, his reputation.

It is no longer merely conjecture to connect the Hollywood Hospital attack with Bradley Robert Edwards' violent escalation to serial murder. We now know that the man who attacked me all those years ago went on to brutally rape and murder other women. I now know that, had circumstances been different, he could easily have done the same to me. Because of the police's and his employer's response to that attack, the behaviour of Bradley Robert Edwards went unchecked, and he was able to go on to become the Claremont serial killer.

Edwards' behaviour in 1990 was clearly abnormal, and should have rung alarm bells. Painful though it may be to revisit old ground, understanding what went wrong back then is crucial to ensuring that we do things differently today. Although it happened many years ago, we need to have this conversation. The Western Australia Police Force needs to have this conversation. Telstra needs to have this conversation. We, as a society, need to have this conversation. We, as women, and men – the most common perpetrators of violence – need to have this conversation.

After I was attacked, I felt unheard, disbelieved, powerless. But if I am honest, my own fear of disparagement, of being labelled 'bothersome', 'attention seeking', even 'hysterical' if I didn't just cope and get on with things, was so ingrained that when the police charged my assailant with a less serious offence than the one he had committed, when Telecom advocated for him, when no-one really listened to me, when no-one encouraged or supported me to push the matter further, I simply let it drop. I lost my voice. I acquiesced to 'the system', to the prevailing order that valued a man's career and wellbeing over a woman's right to safety. As time moved on, I buried the trauma and did what women – particularly women of my generation – were taught to do: I just got on with things. I didn't make a fuss.

As I write this, in early 2021, the world has changed and women everywhere are finding their voices, speaking out, finally making themselves heard, and for this I am grateful. I am proud of them. And I am so relieved.

* * *

The arrest of Edwards in 2016 and the lengthy process of bringing him to justice affected my life in more ways than I could ever have imagined. I am no longer a young woman, and the repeated reliving of the trauma of the attack and its aftermath throughout the long, drawn-out process of the trial had an impact on my personal life. It has caused me emotional distress, and it has had negative consequences for my physical health.

The opportunity to give evidence in the Supreme Court of Western Australia, however, began my catharsis. It set in motion the process of validation that I felt was denied to me all those years ago, and I was grateful for the chance to finally tell my story in a way that could, in some small way, help others. I believe that the prosecution's argument for Edwards' propensity for violence when under emotional stress was made more effective by my firsthand evidence – along with the psychological reports and other corroborating evidence – and I like to think that the prosecution team had come to know me well enough to believe that I would be able to do justice to that evidence.

I also like to think that times have changed – that there is now more of a culture of victim support, of allowing victims of serious crimes a chance to tell their story, to be heard, and I am grateful to the DPP and to Justice Hall for allowing this opportunity in my case.

I am, in fact, grateful for many things. With hindsight and much reflection, I can now see that my terrifying experience all those years ago, while undeniably traumatic, also left me with an underlying feeling of thankfulness just for being alive. The journey of the past five years since Edwards' arrest, while often exhausting and sometimes excruciatingly painful, has absolutely magnified that feeling in me.

The recording of my experiences has unearthed many strong emotions, including feelings of fear, trauma, anger, anxiety, sadness and – undeniably – strong feelings of guilt.

To the families of Sarah Spiers, Jane Rimmer and Ciara Glennon, to the woman who was raped in Karrakatta Cemetery, I need to say to you that I am sorry. I am sorry that I lost my voice, that I was too traumatised at the time to speak out, that I did not manage to fully convey the terror I felt that day, that I did not try to formally challenge the charge, that I doubted myself, that I ultimately just gave up and got on with my own life.

I did my best at the time, but no-one would listen. My only hope is that we are better at listening now.

ACKNOWLEDGEMENTS

Some of the events recorded in this book happened many years ago. My recollections of those times are sometimes very clear and sometimes much hazier. They are my memories, and I have tried to document them accurately.

Much of the trial and pre-trial information detailed in the latter part of this book was gleaned from the many and varied media reports on the case from Western Australia. I would like to thank reporters from the *West Australian* newspaper for keeping me and the Western Australian community informed as the tragic story of the Claremont killings and its aftermath unfolded.

Thank you to the *West Australian* for granting me permission to reproduce material from their reports, and to Penguin Random House for permission to quote material from Debi Marshall's *The Devil's Garden* (2007).

I am appreciative of the understanding and sensitivity shown by the Western Australia Police Force and the Western Australian Office of the Director of Public Prosecutions during the preparations for my court appearance. In particular, Brendan Kelly and Katy, the Special Crime Squad homicide detectives who were assigned to me, and Brad Hollingsworth, the Assistant Deputy Chief Prosecutor, all helped me to feel part of the process in the long months leading up to the trial.

To *60 Minutes* producer Nick Greenaway, thanks for the opportunity to tell my story, and for the wine.

A big thank you also to Georgia Richter at Fremantle Press, who believed in my story enough to take it to print.

To my friends Lucy and Vikki, and editors Fiona Inglis, Kylie Mason and the very patient and talented wordsmith Leila Jabbour: you all helped to turn my diary entries, notes and ramblings into a readable story, and I am grateful.

And, finally, to my husband, Tim, who has been beside me for every step of this harrowing journey, to my daughters Kate, Martha and Jo, to my friend Sheila, to all my family, thank you for your support. I love you dearly.

First published 2022 by
FREMANTLE PRESS

Fremantle Press Inc. trading as Fremantle Press
PO Box 158, North Fremantle, Western Australia, 6159
www.fremantlepress.com.au

Cover images: shutterstock.com: thodonal88, Aleksandr Andrushkiv, PanicAttack.
Designed by Carolyn Brown, tendeersigh.com.au.
Printed by McPherson's Printing, Victoria, Australia.

A catalogue record for this book is available from the National Library of Australia

ISBN 9781760991227 (paperback)
ISBN 9781760991234 (ebook)

Fremantle Press is supported by the State Government through the Department of Local Government, Sport and Cultural Industries

Fremantle Press respectfully acknowledges the Whadjuk people of the Noongar nation as the traditional owners and custodians of the land where we work in Walyalup.